SIX-LEGGED

SEX

The Erotic Lives of Bugs

JAMES K. WANGBERG

Illustrations by Marjorie C. Leggitt

Fulcrum Publishing
Golden, Colorado

To my former and current students

Library of Congress Cataloging-in-Publication Data
Wangberg, James K. (James Keith)
  Six-legged sex : the erotic lives of bugs / James K. Wangberg ;
illustrations by Marjorie C. Leggitt.
      p. cm.
Includes bibliographical references and index.
  ISBN 1-55591-292-3 (pbk.)
  1. Insects—Behavior. 2. Sexual behavior in animals.
  3. Insects—Behavior—Humor. 4. Sexual behavior in animals—Humor.
  I. Title.
QL496 .W37 2001
595.7156'2—dc21

                              2001002336

Printed in the United States of America
0 9 8 7 6 5 4 3 2 1

Editorial: Marlene Blessing, Alex Goulder, Daniel Forrest-Bank
Cover and interior design: Elizabeth Watson

Fulcrum Publishing
16100 Table Mountain Parkway, Suite 300
Golden, Colorado 80403
(800) 992-2908 • (303) 277-1623
www.fulcrum-books.com

Contents

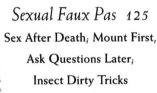

Acknowledgments

Several individuals assisted me with this project and I am pleased to acknowledge them. I am grateful to these former colleagues in the University of Wyoming Center for Teaching Excellence (CTE) for helping me select the book title: Andrew Bryson, Joseph Gregg, Patricia Hutchings, and Jane Nelson. Thanks too, to former CTE secretary Cheryl Hageman for her clerical assistance. Jane Nelson also deserves my special thanks for her careful reviews of manuscript drafts, her constructive edits, and for her encouragement throughout the project. I am deeply appreciative of the clerical support and computer assistance provided by my current secretary, Pepper Jo Six. Tonya Talbert offered excellent professional advice on some of the writing and I am grateful for her shared enthusiasm for the book. Another enthusiastic supporter who helped make the project possible was my former dean, Steven Horn, whose own writing is an inspiration for me.

Special thanks and acknowledgment must go to my entomology colleagues for lending their expertise and constructive criticisms during various phases of the project. John George and Jay McPherson were most helpful in editing and reacting to the text. I benefited from their corrections as well as their suggestions for content and additional sources of information. Another entomology colleague, Richard Hurley, provided ideas for chapters from the onset of the project and was a continual source of encouragement. He, too, provided valuable suggestions and edits to the manuscript.

To all of the entomologists and other scientists who have contributed to the scientific literature on which this book is based, I salute you.

Lastly, I am grateful for the continuing support I receive from all of my family, Lesley, Michelle, Stephanie, and Ryan. Their encouragement, love, pride, and patience are pillars for me.

Introduction

Almost as much by chance as by design I discovered the
fascinating and at times bizarre world of insect behavior while
studying biology in college. The things that these six-legged
creatures were said to do were more than enough to capture my
interest, not the least of which were their sexual habits. That early
fascination with insect behavior led to a wonderfully fulfilling
career in entomology as a university teacher, researcher, and now
administrator. Much of my early research focused on insect natural
history, which entailed countless hours of observing insect behaviors,
including their most intimate acts. My active research in these areas
tapered off several years ago, but I remain involved by reading the
scientific literature and keeping in touch with colleagues. It is a
privilege to be a part of the scientific community, to be able to
share in the latest discoveries about insect life, and to remain
connected with others worldwide investigating and writing about
insect habits.

Sometimes, however, it seems unfortunate that the exciting
stories revealed by scientists are only shared among ourselves. Our
scientific vocabulary and the highly technical aspect of our profession
exclude those not educated in the disciplines. Some aspects of
scientific work are popularized and made more understandable to
lay audiences, but there is still so much information that remains
hidden in scientific literature, accessible only to relatively few.
This book was written to let others in on some of these secrets.

The stories contained herein are my interpretations and
translations of articles in scientific journals and in science books.

The sources are cited at the end of the book. Most of the articles and books that are cited are highly technical, and probably of limited interest to the lay reader, but nonetheless provide much greater detail about the chapter topics. One source (*The Evolution of Insect Mating Systems* by Thornhill and Alcock) is cited frequently as it contains a wealth of information on the evolution of insect reproductive behavior. I recommend this book to the reader who wishes to explore the serious scientific literature dealing with insect sexual behaviors.

I have endeavored to be accurate and not misrepresent scientific theories and facts contained in the literature, but I remain responsible for any errors that may not have been seen or corrected. I must also plead guilty to something that scientists abhor: being anthropocentric. I confess that this book takes great liberty in speaking about insects as if they were human and often in human terms. I have done so deliberately in order to help the reader better relate to organisms that otherwise may seem totally alien, and to have fun with the subject at hand. Do not conclude from my loose use of anthropocentric language that insects and related creatures should be assigned interesting human characteristics. They are sufficiently interesting in their own right.

Lastly, in the contemporary movie world there are labels alerting viewers to movies that may be suitable for mature audiences only. Perhaps this book deserves an "R" rating, or at least a "PG-13." It contains adult language, sexual content, nudity, and violence. But such is the nature of the animal world. At least I can assure you that the sex and violence is not of the gratuitous kind. It is matter-of-fact, and meant to be educational as well as entertaining. Enjoy six-legged sex—vicariously.

1

Powerful Aphrodisiacs
and Other Insect Love Potions

Aphrodisiacs are chemicals that stimulate a strong sexual response
in insects, humans, or other creatures. They can be thought of
as powerful love potions or perfumes, and insects have been
manufacturing them for millions of years. In the insect world the
perfumes used by the sexes to lure their mates are called pheromones.
It is no coincidence that a human perfume company has released
a product with the trademarked name Pheromone.

The Scent of a Woman

Female moths, which are among the most famous sex pheromone producers, emit pheromone puffs and plumes like an aerosol spray that drifts with the wind, hopefully in the direction of a sexually primed adult male. There are some remarkable insects that produce pheromone sprays visible to the naked eye, but most insects release their perfumes in the most minute quantities, quantities that are very difficult to detect and analyze even with the most sophisticated scientific equipment. Moth sex pheromones are measured in picograms and nanograms (Phelan 1997). A nano is a billionth. A pico is a trillionth. A gram equals .03527 ounces. Therefore we are talking about hundred-billionths and hundred-trillionths of an ounce of insect perfume. If, like humans, insects purchased their perfume by the ounce, imagine how long it would last.

In spite of these incomprehensibly low amounts, the perfume is extremely potent. The tiniest whiff can turn an insect into a single-minded sex addict. A male moth can detect a virgin female's odor at great distances. Smelling a picogram of perfume at its source seems like a miraculous sense of smell, but male moths are able to catch the scent after it has drifted in the wind for over a mile! They not only recognize the smell of a virgin, but they are able to distinguish her perfume from that produced by sexually incompatible moths of other species. Males navigate in zigzag flights against the wind in order to continually cross the perfumed air trail and systematically close in on their potential mates.

When a male gets in close proximity to his perfumed partner, his eyesight becomes more important, and he navigates the final distance to her visually. Some males have their own pheromone or cologne that appeals to the female. Her scent serves as an attractant, and his scent serves as an aphrodisiac. With all of this perfume in the air, both are more eager to engage in sex.

Insects manufacture their pheromones by virtue of their own special biochemistry and they possess special glands for storing the potent compounds and for releasing them into the environment at the proper time. Some insects obtain chemicals from the plants on which they feed, to manufacture a concoction of insect-derived and plant-derived chemical perfume. As distasteful as it sounds, some insect perfumes, like those of bark beetles, are a combination of all these chemicals and their own frass, or solid wastes.

There are also so-called antiaphrodisiacs in the insect world. Some insect males may produce their own powerful scent, which they conveniently leave on the body of the female after mating with her. Tainted with the odor of a male, she is no longer recognizable as a sexy female; consequently other males seeking a sex partner bypass her on their mating quest.

Spanishfly

One insect has become notorious as a human aphrodisiac. It is called the Spanishfly, not really a fly but a member of a family of beetles called the blister beetles. Blister beetles are aptly named because they secrete an irritating and toxic chemical called cantharidin. This chemical acts in the beetle's defense by oozing from its joints and causing a burning sensation and blisters when it comes in contact with an animal's skin. Horse owners are especially mindful of the blistering effects of these beetles,

Spanishfly my eye! I'm a blister beetle.

because just a few live or dead blister beetles in a horse's hay can cause extreme swelling and inflammation in the esophagus, and in some cases will kill the horse.

Why would an insect that can kill horses and burn and blister human skin gain a reputation as an aphrodisiac? It doesn't sound like something to use for a massage let alone something to eat or drink. Nonetheless such dubious use is documented in history. Berenbaum (1995) tells of the prosecution of the famous Marquis de Sade in 1772 for poisoning prostitutes while trying to sneak a dose of Spanishfly to "inflame their passions." It has been rumored that some believe a topical dose of ground blister beetle to the genitals will act as a strong aphrodisiac. Such an act is more likely to inflame one's genitals before one's passions. Stick to candlelight and romantic music. Leave the cantharidin to the beetles.

2

Love Songs and Serenades

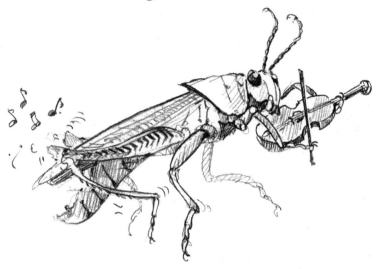

Male insects rank among the world's best crooners. The serenading skills and love songs of such insects as crickets, grasshoppers, katydids, and cicadas are the most famous and, to their female counterparts, simply irresistible. Many other insects, less known for their singing ability, are equally adept at attracting sexual partners with special melodies. They include beetles, moths, water bugs, planthoppers, flies, ants, termites, and others. With such a rich ensemble of singing insects, it is no wonder that the types of songs, musical instruments, and orchestral methods are equally diverse.

Insect Violins and Harps

First, consider the types of musical instruments that insects possess

and the manner in which they sing. The most common musical
instrument is composed of paired structures commonly referred to
as the scraper and file. As the names imply, the scraper is a device
that rubs against a roughened file and the repetitious friction
between the two creates a vibration, which to the insect ear is
a sexual melody. Entomologists call this *stridulation*. The song doesn't
come from the mouth and a voicebox, but rather from these tools
which may be on legs, wings, or other adjacent body parts. Humans
may hear the *chirp, chirp, chirp* of the cricket or the piercing screech
of the cicada, but the female of those species hears the insect
equivalent of Frank Sinatra.

The grasshoppers typically have the scraper on their inner
"thigh," which they rub against the file on the nearby wing, a crude
but effective violin. Crickets actually have a portion of a wing that's
called a harp, which produces the call when the scraper on one
wing rubs the file on the other wing. Some katydids have scraper
and file mechanisms associated with the upper
lip, so in fact they sing with their mouthparts,
an unusual and nontraditional use of an
insect's oral apparatus.

A Singing Penis

Singing with one's legs and/or wings or
orally is not nearly as bizarre, however,
as singing with one's genitals! This
is the serenading mode for a few
moths and a certain water boatman
(a common water bug). The male's genitalia

*Some water boatman
have a singing penis*

are beautifully equipped as organs for sexual intercourse
and as singing devices. Male moths equipped with such
fancy musical instruments perch with genitals exposed and project

their unique song. These sexual singing instruments with associated resonators are said to produce near pure tone ultrasonic signals.

Insect Percussionists

Some male insects and certain spiders are percussionists. Stonefly males bang their bodies against the ground and actually drum to attract mates. Some wolf spider females are attracted to the most active male drummers. Male wolf spiders drum on dry leaves and in so doing communicate to females their viability and suitability as fathers. Some male moths have well-developed structures, called *castanets*, on their wings that bang with each wing beat, establishing a unique love rhythm. Many insects produce inaudible pulses of air as a result of elaborate wing displays or wing vibrations; they are inaudible to humans but detectable by highly sensitive hairs on receptive females. If having hairs sensitive enough to detect the air movements of insect wings sounds far-fetched, consider the fact reported in Bailey (1991) that the anal hairs on a cockroach can detect the on-rushing tongue of a toad!

One of the great insect percussionists is the male cicada, equipped with two powerful tymbals that produce a screeching love-call for female cicadas in much the same way as theaters use a sheet of metal to create the sound of thunder. The tymbals are contained within a large air chamber for resonating the sound, and muscles cause them to bow and flex rapidly,

Male cicadas make good vibrations

generating their distinctive vibration. However, sometimes there can be problems. Unfortunately for the cicada, some manmade sounds can interfere with insect lovemaking and create what would be embarrassing situations, if insects could be embarrassed. For instance, it is not uncommon for the drone of a gasoline-powered lawn mower engine to mimic the pitch and frequency of a calling cicada male. Hence, stimulated female cicadas with sexual intentions may dive-bomb revving engines instead of serenading males. It must be confusing, and likely painful, for the lovesick female to alight on a Briggs & Stratton.

Insect Duets, Choruses, and Ballads

The proper role for males in the insect world is to sing and attract the female, while the female's role is to be coy. Hence, males usually possess the musical instruments and females do not. However, some females, upon hearing the calling male, will respond with a song of their own, and insect duets are born. Duetting is common as female and male crickets converge on one another. Once physical contact has been made, the male may continue to sing. But he will sing a different tune and sing more softly to keep the female's attention through foreplay and mating. If cricket lovemaking is interrupted by unwanted guests then the male's song changes once again to a tune that signals *coitus interruptus*. His loving serenade will resume when the interruption has ceased.

Insect choruses are sometimes formed when many male crickets of the same species sing together. However, males typically keep safe distances from one another when chorusing, minimizing competition for mates. Such cricket choirs seem particularly effective in luring females, presumably because of the louder call and multiplicity of attractive males. Some mole crickets, which burrow in the mud, construct tunnels in such a way as to amplify their sound and broadcast their song from double exits that act like dual megaphones. Other insects carefully select sites high atop vegetation to ensure their songs are heard over the greatest distance. A snowy tree cricket constructs its own echo chamber by properly chewing leaves, which serve as strong internal baffles for projecting its song.

Mole crickets are love megaphones

Male songs, whether solo acts or done as a choir, can properly be defined as ballads. They tell a story. For example, the male insect ballad conveys to females his identity. Females of one species are not attracted to males of a different kind or to those not genetically compatible. Scientists also surmise that the ballad tells the female about his physical condition. She can determine from the serenade if he is in good health and if he is free of any bad mutations. She can detect his social standing from his song, which might mean that he possesses property (territory), he is strong and aggressive, and he has the skills to gather resources (is a good provider). For every singing species there is a specific song and mode of singing. While scientists may not always recognize the difference in appearance between one species and another, the different musical repertoire will segregate species every time. Judging by the numbers of crickets and other insect songsters, it seems safe to say that the insects have no difficulty recognizing their preferred music.

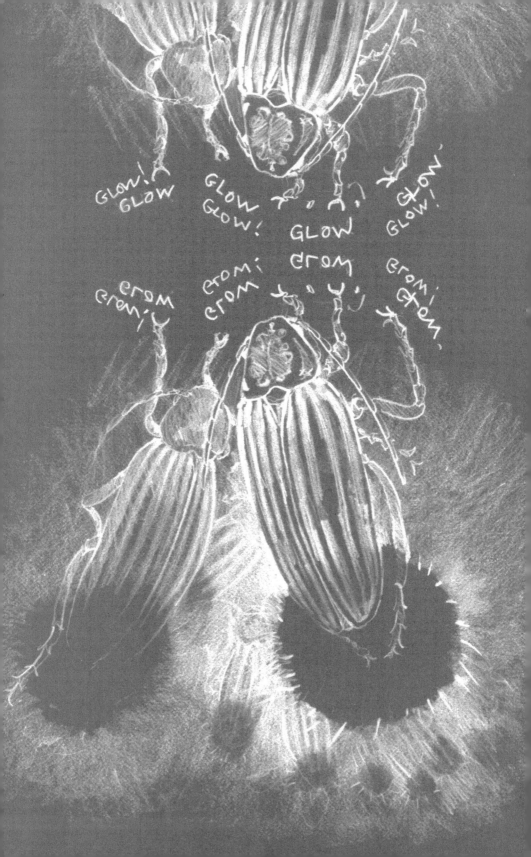

3

You Light My Fire:
Insect Flashers

GLOW! GLOW GLOW GLOW GLOW GLOW! GLOW GLOW! GLOW GLOW!

*As the sun sets and twilight gives way to darkness, fireflies around
the world do what they do best to attract mates. They produce lights
that ignite fellow fireflies' passions. Fireflies are not flies as their name
implies, but rather beetles in a family named Lampyridae. As this*

Latin name suggests, lampyrids possess lamps or lanterns on their rear ends, which, thanks to the magic of chemistry, produce a cold light when two chemicals, luciferin and luciferase (after Lucifer or Satan), are combined. Fireflies are not the only organisms in the world that are bioluminescent. There are other light-producing insects, and many sea creatures and bacteria have glowing properties too. But the fireflies are perhaps the most intriguing because of the intricate ways they use their lighted lanterns for sexual enticement.

Don't Dim the Lights

Unlike the serenading insects, in which males typically beckon females nearer with their melodies, both male and female fireflies may light up the sky as a sexual prelude. However, when a male firefly lights his love torch, it is not to lure a female closer, but rather to elicit a flashing reply from her so he can recognize her and know her whereabouts. The flashes of fireflies are in fact quite complex and comprise an intricate pattern of love calls. Each firefly species has its own characteristic flash and flashing pattern, which typically varies by color, intensity of the flash, rate of flashing, and the duration of the flash. For instance, fireflies that prefer the twilight time for sex favor yellowish light, while late-night lovemakers prefer greenish hues. There are also specific flashing sites on or off the ground and heights in the air or on vegetation that various species prefer. The combination of all these factors creates a rich repertoire for firefly species. The repertoire is enriched further when some firefly species flash in harmony and in synchrony.

A single ground-dwelling firefly male may begin a sort of flashing harmony by triggering with his flash a series of flashes, by as many as 60 other males, along a line of sight on the ground. The resultant flash train is said to resemble miniature lightning bolts as the train of males synchronizes flashes with others in a follow-the-leader style. Among the most spectacular examples of synchronous flashers are some Southeast Asian firefly species and their "beacon trees." These fireflies flash in perfect synchrony and in large communal displays, appearing like lights on a Christmas tree. Sometimes an individual male in one of these huge communal light shows gets distracted and will steer his attention away from synchronous flashing males and direct his beam of light toward a female that he has detected in the distance. Laboratory experiments have

Flashing is acceptable among fireflies

revealed that this species can be distracted in other ways too. These hedonistic firefly males, when placed in front of mirrors, can be observed flashing at themselves.

There is also a collection of firefly species that prefers a solo act of cruising habitats while flashing, to elicit a flash response from a female. There is one such species in New Guinea, called the surf zone firefly, which patrols the narrow shoreline between the surf spray zone and the neighboring jungle, flashing for his mate. Apparently the moonlit beach and pounding surf can be romantic for insects too.

Insect Fatal Attractions

The firefly story is incomplete without the fatal attraction saga, or what has been labeled insect *femmes fatales*. While the majority of fireflies use flashing to facilitate a sexual rendezvous, some fireflies have hostile, not reproductive, motives. A firefly female named *Photurus* is a predaceous species and she is not above eating other fireflies. To accomplish this

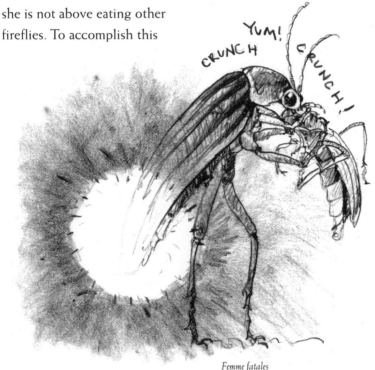

Femme fatales

macabre act, she mimics the flashing pattern of female fireflies of a group named *Photinus*. Unsuspecting *Photinus* males interpret the flashing *Photurus* as their potential mate and fly to her with amorous intent. Into her waiting legs *Photinus* will fly, discovering too late that the attractive flash was a deadly imitation. When *Photurus* females are in the mood for love, they change their flashing pattern to one recognized by *Photurus* males, thereby attracting proper mates to satisfy their sexual appetites—as opposed to their appetite for food.

These predatory fireflies with copycat flashes are common in North America. Hence, the evening sky is a site of seduction and danger to the myriad of flashing males in search of females. The search for females with a sexual appetite can result in finding a female with simply an appetite. However, recent studies have revealed that the deceptive predator *Photurus* gains more than a nutritious meal by eating a fellow firefly. The female *Photurus* is also ingesting a steroid chemical contained in her prey that is repulsive to some of her chief predators, spiders and birds. It is a chemical similar to the venom of certain toads and not at all tasty. Therefore, *Photurus* females that have eaten steroid-laden *Photinus* males are rejected by jumping spiders that would otherwise eagerly consume them. *Photurus* females seem to have the best of both worlds. They get to eat what to some would be noxious-tasting prey, and in return become repulsive to their own would-be predators, living another day to dine on another duped *Photinus* male.

4

Dirty Dancing
and Sexual Foreplay

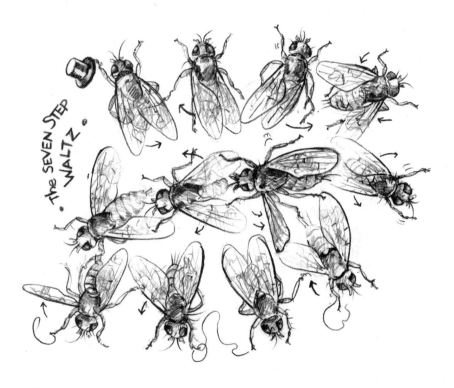

*S*ex for some insects starts at the dance. And like people, some insects are better dancers than others. Some must dance, and dance well, in order to fulfill their ultimate sexual goals. An entire family of flies has earned the name dance flies because of their special courtship dancing talent. The dance steps can be intricate and they may include more *than just the insect's feet. Insect dances often involve wings, antennae, mouthparts, and subtle as well as not so subtle body movements. Insect dances often lead toward sexual foreplay or are sometimes accompanied by foreplay. Some dances may be low-key with hardly any sexual overtones, something like a proper ballroom dance. Others can be wild and erotic, the insect equivalent of the Brazilian lambada or Hollywood's* Dirty Dancing.

Dressing for the Big Dance

A lot of insects are dressed for the dance. That is, they possess special colors and markings on the wings that serve as signals exciting to their dancing partners. Good examples of insects with special adornments, that are also skilled dancers, are the picture-winged flies and fruit flies. Sometimes referred to as the peacock flies, these species display showy wing colors and can really strut their stuff, not unlike a male peacock. I am particularly fond of the fruit flies because of the amount of attention I gave them in research several years ago. Without their permission, I observed their most intimate moments under natural field conditions and while they were confined in cages in the laboratory. I was interested in all aspects of their lives, but their sex lives were of special interest, because

Fruit fly males box for mates

knowledge of their sexual behavior would help unlock some secrets about their identities and ecological roles.

The fruit flies that I observed are a bit smaller than a house fly and they have distinctive dark patterns on their wings: bands, stripes, and spots. A person familiar with fruit fly wing patterns can tell one species from another, but sorting some species can be difficult. Presumably the fruit flies themselves have an easier time of it, because conspicuous wing displays are part of their courtship dancing repertoire and they are very alert to each other's conspicuous designs and dances.

Basic Dance Steps

The fruit fly courtship dance has seven required steps. If any one step is omitted, then the sexual encounter ends or must start over. If any of the seven steps are performed badly, then that too ruins the mood and the couple must go back to square one. Step One: Males and females initiate the dance by walking about in apparently random fashion, eventually closing the distance between each other. As they walk, they may display their wings in various manners. Both wings may twitch forward simultaneously. Both wings may slide together across the body to the left and to the right, or each wing may be held outstretched one at a time, with its full surface turned at a right angle to give an onlooking fly a full view of its beautiful color. This last wing display is like a sailor signaling with semaphores. This leads to Step Two, eye contact.

The fruit flies seem nonchalant during much of the dance, often taking time out to rest or to groom themselves. Any respectable fruit fly doesn't want to appear too eager, so standing around in casual fashion, grooming legs, wings, and antennae, seems like a good dating strategy. At some point fruit fly coyness turns into fruit fly passion and this leads to Step Three, body language. The two sexes orient toward each other, each proudly displaying their wings. Now the female plays more the role of attention-getter and the male becomes the more active pursuer. The male initiates Step Four, the approach, and with wings waving and legs dancing, he attempts to go from a fast dance to the slow dance, with physical touch. This step may have to be repeated several times because many females play hard to get, breaking away from the dance and forcing the male to ask again or to seek a new partner. If successful, however, the male makes it to Step Five, physical contact. Usually this entails the male gently tapping his female partner's body with his front legs, a fly's polite way of asking for the slow dance. In some instances these courtship dances begin as same-sex encounters and two males rise up and "box" each other with their front legs. If all continues to go well, the male literally makes the jump to Step Six, mounting the female. This can be a turn-off for the female and many a male faces rejection, but when the dance has gone well and the chemistry between fruit fly couples is right, then sexual foreplay becomes more obvious.

Insect Kissing and Petting

Sexual foreplay involves continued male tapping and stroking of the female's body with his legs and feet. There is also fruit fly kissing. The male "kisses" the female's body with his outstretched mouthparts. His mouthparts rythmically go in and out, caressing the female from above. In another family of fruit flies, there is much heavier "petting," as males lick the female's genitals (Spieth 1968). This type of foreplay is important in keeping the female interested and aroused, and eventually leads to the ultimate Step Seven, consummation.

The male maneuvers his genitalia to unite with the female's organs and they remain in their sexual union for a couple of hours.

The "kissing" continues throughout the sex act, and seems to be important in maintaining a meaningful relationship. Afterward, both sexes spend time resting and grooming, but to date none has been observed smoking a cigarette.

There are countless other examples of insect courtship dances and foreplay, and they typically involve a wide range of cues including touch, odor, appearance, and sounds. Depending upon the insect species, many different body parts come into play. One grasshopper species has been reported to use seven different parts of its body in its courtship and mating (Otte 1972), a sensual species indeed.

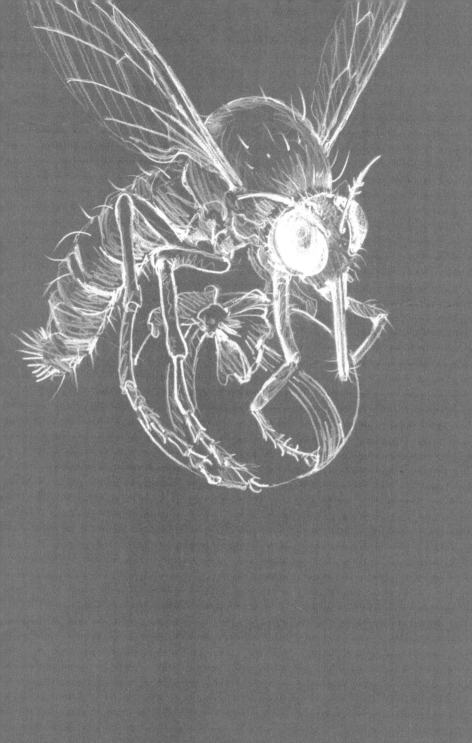

5

Do Not Open
Before Sex

In the world of flies, there are others besides the contemptible house fly, the biting flies and mosquitoes, and the numerous other gnats and midges that frequently bother us and invade our space. There are, for example, those romantic dance flies, named for the intricate and seductive dance patterns males use to lure their mates.

The more common run-of-the-mill dance fly uses its own particular dance repertoire, with twists and turns and aerobatic maneuvers, to entice females nearer and ultimately into a sexual embrace. But there are some other dance flies, also called balloon flies (*Hilara*), that have taken romance to a higher level: higher in the sense of complex behavior, but not higher if one imagines an insect code of ethics or morality.

Nuptial Gifts

Consider three species of *Hilara* (referred to by number for simplicity). A species one male captures a small insect prey as a nuptial gift (the equivalent of a box of chocolates) for his potential mate. With this tempting morsel dangling in full view of some virgin female, the male dances his dance and waves his wings, until the female can no longer resist. She joins him in a balloon fly's sexual bliss. While she feasts on the tasty treat, he obtains his prize, sex. The time that she takes to feed is the time the male requires to complete the sex act and fertilize her eggs. The happy couple then go about their separate ways.

Species two has refined this act to be a bit more romantic. Like species one, he dances, waves his wings, and brings a "box of chocolates," but, in a nice added touch, he takes the time to wrap his present with a tidy ball of silk before offering it to her. The female, equally enticed by the dancing, wing waving, and now the lure of a wrapped present, joins the male for sex. As she unwraps the gift, he does his thing, and by the time the present is unwrapped and the morsel eaten, there has been even more time for the male and female to have sex.

Now enters species three, who has, from a male dance fly point of view, come up with the best get-sex strategy yet devised. He too offers his virgin what appears to be a gift enticingly wrapped in silk as he dances and waves. Equally excited, the female embraces him for sex and proceeds to unwrap her gift. It takes just as long as it did for species two, so the sex act does not get cut short; however, when the female finishes unwrapping her gift, she discovers (you guessed it) an empty package.

I leave it to you to decide what the moral of this story might be.

6

But Will You
Respect Me in the Morning?

*B*efore anyone becomes too self-righteous or judgmental about respectful behaviors between the sexes in insects, consider the numerous examples of insect sex in which the male remains with his mate long after the act. Instances of prolonged association may serve a variety of purposes.

Feed Me, Cuddle Me

Sometimes males remain *in copula*, sex organs fully engaged, well after the period in which sperm are transferred and eggs fertilized. They do so not as chastity belts (see Chapter 16), although their prolonged intimacy certainly serves that purpose, but rather to provide some special nourishment to the female. Many male insects, like certain

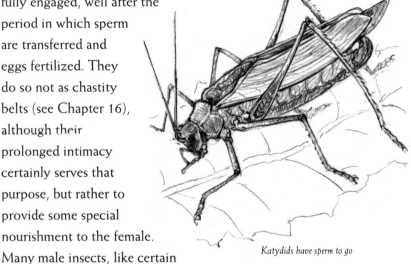

Katydids have sperm to go

katydids, package their sperm in convenient parcels or sperm packets. The sperm packets contain more than seminal fluid and sperm. They contain rich nutrients. Because the male remains in a prolonged sexual embrace with the female, she is able to receive the supplemental food, which may increase her egg production and presumably the viability of her offspring.

Another purpose is closely related to the insect chastity belt phenomenon. Some insects, following sex and disengagement of the sex organs, will remain a "couple" because the male insists on clinging to his mate; perhaps the insect version of cuddling. In so doing, the male deters others looking for their opportunity to mate with the same female. One example is the tiger beetle, whose male, with prominent sickle-like jaws, grasps his mate in his jaws and travels with her for a prolonged period after the sex act. This is certainly a far cry from the insensitive male of some species who leaves the female and exits the scene immediately following his sexual conquest. Other mate-grasping behavior is found among different beetles, flies, and the water striders (those common expert skaters on the water's surface).

Protect Me

Male insect chivalry may extend toward their offspring too, beginning with oviposition or egg-laying activities of mated females. Many dragonfly and damselfly males, following physical separation from their mates, will remain nearby and patrol the best egg-laying habitats to increase the females' chances of successful egg-laying and to frighten away any other males with naughty intentions.

Males may remain with their partners for long periods to protect them from marauding predators too. It is a good scientific guess that by doing so males not only assist females as they seek premium egg-laying sites, but the extra assistance allows females some protection to feed and to care for their offspring. One water strider, reported by Arnqvist (1997), may deserve recognition as the most loyal male. He remains with his mate and guards her after sex for several weeks, longer than some adult insect lifetimes.

Male water striders are loyal mates

A male particularly helpful in protecting the offspring, and certainly one of the best insect examples of fatherhood, is the fierce giant water bug. This creature, a large water-dwelling insect, possesses a piercing beak capable of delivering a painful bite to people, and a fatal blood-draining and tissue-dissolving bite to other insects, tadpoles, frogs, and small fish. It is intimidating indeed. What better place for the female to deposit her eggs than on the back of her mate? The male giant water bug carries her eggs glued tightly to his back, where they remain until the hatchlings emerge and swim off to fend for themselves.

Male giant water bugs have a gentler side

He is more than a convenient site for attaching eggs. He will do "push-ups" near the water surface, which helps maintain necessary oxygen levels for his developing offspring.

Finally, another reason for males to remain with their mates is more self-serving. Many insects mate more than once, and the males of these species may simply remain *in copula* or grasp the female for the duration between matings. The male stays with his mate until he's ready to do it again, insuring his own sexual success and guarding against insect infidelity.

7

Boys in the 'Hood

*I*nsect neighborhoods are not that different from our own neighborhoods. There are good ones and there are bad ones. For species of territorial grasshoppers, the good neighborhoods contain high-quality shrubs—plants that provide good shelter for the resting grasshopper and, most importantly, plants that provide excellent nutrition for the hungry grasshopper. What may appear to us to be two shrubs of the same kind, to a grasshopper may be as different as New York's Fifth Avenue and any city's skid row. One shrub, the prime real estate, is rich in carbohydrates, proteins, and vitamins that grasshoppers can detect. The second shrub, or poor real estate, may look good on the outside but it lacks the necessary amenities for grasshoppers. Competition for the prime real estate is keen among bachelor grasshoppers, because their success in attracting mates is directly related to the quality of housing they are able to offer.

Location, Location, Location!

No self-respecting virgin female grasshopper will be found in a bad neighborhood. Bachelor males see to that. The males stake claim to the finest real estate, perching on high-quality shrubs and sending the most energetic calls that they can, advertising their recent property purchase. They rub together their special musical instruments, located on their wings and legs, and in so doing advertise to other males that this is their turf. The song is also a signal to aid females in finding the finest real estate. Thus, within an area containing thousands of shrubs, the equivalent of a grasshopper city comprising different quality housing and neighborhoods, there may be thousands of bachelor grasshoppers singing praises to the quality of their property and to their sexual prowess.

Virgin females are strongly attracted to sexy sounding males who own nice property, and females avidly seek them out. The rewards are not superficial, however, because engagements between females and wealthy property owners will yield greater benefits for the young mother-to-be's offspring. By residing in the best neighborhood, the female gets a nutritional package that translates into more eggs, larger eggs, and faster-maturing eggs, and the male and female grasshoppers are able to produce a large and strong next generation. The poor neighborhoods are simply not good places to raise a family.

Fighting for the 'Hood

Males aggressively defend their neighborhoods and the rights of insect matrimony. The successful male and leader of the 'hood is usually the first one to stake claim to the prime real estate. To keep his claim requires vigorous singing. Being larger than competing males doesn't hurt either. If a male is challenged in the 'hood, there will be aggressive displays involving louder singing and the showing off of body parts, like comparing leg sizes. Apparently having bigger biceps or longer legs matters between male grasshoppers. The dominant male will attempt to chase away intruders, and ultimately fights can break out. Grasshoppers are not clean fighters. They wrestle, kick, and bite. Fortunately, grasshopper fights rarely result in death or serious injury. The dominant male maintains his property rights and the conjugal visits that accompany them.

The hapless bachelors that lose fights or who are warded off by stronger males are relegated to living in the insect ghettos. Some may be permitted to reside on the outskirts of the good neighborhood, under the careful watch of the stud grasshopper, but their chance of scoring sexually is essentially zero until they can win over the neighborhood or find a new 'hood of their own. Don't think that the weaker male can sneak in and take over when the leader of the 'hood is gone either! The dominant male, who for whatever reason must leave the

Stud grasshopper

shrub for awhile, does not have difficulty finding his way home. He will quickly reclaim his property rights, control of the neighborhood, and the privilege of luring more virgin females to his turf.

8

Insect Sex Hangouts

*S*ome insects have their own favorite hangouts for picking up members of the opposite sex. Some of these sites are quite popular and many insects choose to gather there. Other hot spots are less obvious, perhaps, for the more discreet sex-seeking bug. In either case, knowing where to look can be the key to successful insect sexual encounters. The encounter sites are very much like those of the more familiar sage grouse, famous from many television nature shows. The male sage grouse parade about in sagebrush territories called leks, puffing their *breasts and displaying colorful feathers, all for the amorous look of a mate. Insect leks are not too different. The territory types vary according to the likes and dislikes of the specific insect.*

Hilltop Parking and Lovers' Lane

A large beelike fly called a *bot*, known to parasitize rats and rabbits, prefers romantic hilltops and mountains as lek sites to cruise for partners. Like some other insects, it is a so-called "hilltopping" species. Long before teenagers discovered favorite spots to park, overlooking romantic city lights, bot flies were congregating in similar locations for much the same purpose. The male bot prefers to fly toward some prominent hilltop or scenic mountain ridge and hang out with other males in hopes that an eligible female will come by. In a scientific article titled "Sex and the bachelor bot," Catts (1994) revealed the previously hidden sex life of these amazing flies. In what might be thought of as the insect equivalent of the bar scene, or the daytime equivalent of an insect lovers' lane, eligible bachelor bots park themselves and stake out territories on prominent hilltops overlooking the countryside, while remaining vigilant to approaching virgin female bots. Other bachelors that infringe upon a rival's territory will be chased from the area. In heavily populated sites, these chases may be by bachelor bot gangs. It is rare for actual fights to break out; however, there are other insects where rival males get into airborne clashes, smacking wings against one another, all for the love of the girl.

Male–female sexual pursuits take place as soon as a virgin bot appears on the scene. Females are conspicuous as they fly into the hilltop territories, cruising just above the tops of the dense brush-covered hill. The vigilant bachelor bot, upon spotting the newly arrived female, immediately takes chase. His is a no-nonsense approach with no time for courtship, gifts, or foreplay. Couples typically embrace at once and bot lovemaking rapidly ensues in the shade and privacy of the dense underbrush. Apparently, even among parasitic bot flies, there is a preference to have sex in seclusion, away from onlookers.

Lonely Vigils—Males in Waiting

There are sexual hangouts popular with other insects too and not always on the tops of hills. Males of other flies and certain bees may perch on prominent sites such as trees, grasses, shrubs, ferns, and fungi. Clearings in forests and fields may be as popular with these insects as the more scenic hilltops are with others. These males are as alert to rival males and to virgin females as their bot fly insect cousins and exhibit many of the same territory defense and mate pursuit behaviors as the bot flies. One wasp, called the tarantula hawk because of its predatory feeding on tarantula spiders, is such an insect. Males perch atop desert vegetation in what is often a very lonely vigil for the rarely seen virgin tarantula hawk (Thornhill and Alcock 1983). It is likely that a male-in-waiting will encounter more male tarantula hawks before it encounters a female, and, hence, rival males end up in frantic chases about the territory. A male tarantula hawk chase can go round and round or spiral out of sight, high into the air, and repeat itself many times before a male establishes dominance and control over the territory. Having done so, the dominant male, usually the larger of the rivals,

A tarantula hawk perched for sex

resumes his lonely vigil perched on a prominent branch and awaits the next insect intruder, hopefully a virgin tarantula hawk.

The next time you are annoyed by buzzing flies or an aggressive wasp at a picnic, whether it is on a scenic hilltop or in a field clearing, consider the possibility that you are the greater intruder. While the insects may have disturbed your quiet time with nature, you may have interrupted or prevented their most intimate moments together.

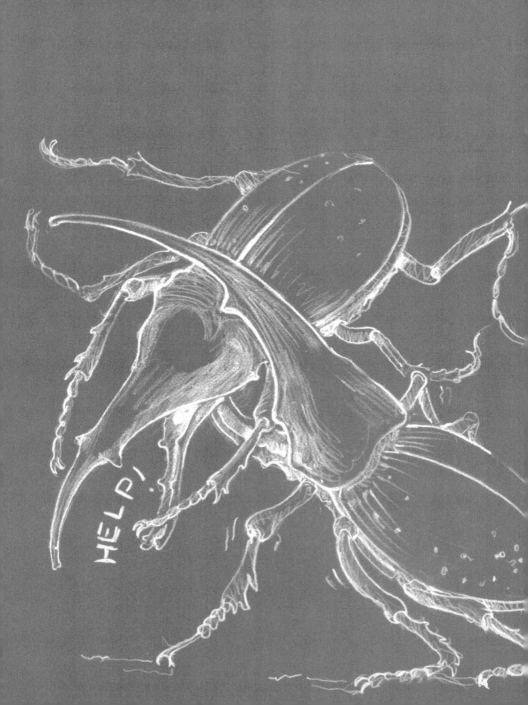

9

I'll Show You Mine
If You'll Show Me Yours

If female and male insects were to compare their sexual anatomies, many would have to show off more than just their genitals, because the differences can extend beyond the organs that they use for mating. Differences may be evident in their antennae, eyes, legs, wings, and colors, as well as their bodies' shapes, sizes, and accessories.

Horny Insects

Some of the best sexually accessorized insects are the horny insect species. Famous for their horns are the giant scarab beetles, some called rhinoceros beetles because the males have huge horns near their heads. They could easily be considered the insect equivalent of the triceratops dinosaur. The horns give the beetle a ferocious look and they are used as jousting weapons when males vie for mates. The male with the largest horns has the best chance to topple or push aside competing males who are less well endowed.

Bite Me, Pinch Me

Beetles not favored with horns may instead have the advantage of gigantic jaws. Most spectacular among these are the stag beetles, also aptly named, because the powerful, grasping jaws, which jut out from their faces, may actually be longer than the beetle's entire body. In the stag beetle world, such jaws might win a female by being as overpowering to a competing male as a large antler rack would be in the mating games of stag elk.

Earwigs are insects that prefer approaching combat from the rear. They are notable for the accessories attached at the hind end. Earwigs have large pincers on their rears and the males of some species have pincers larger than what a modest earwig might consider normal. The pincers may look more dangerous to people than they really are; however, the best-endowed males are capable of delivering a painful pinch, especially to tender skin. In addition to self-defense, the male's large pincers are used in combating male rivals.

Feelers and Other Sex Gear

Other insect contestants show off their differences with fancy or enlarged antennae, and some tiny wasps and midges actually use their antennae like arms to grasp female partners. But the insect males with the greatest bragging rights for fancy antennae, compared to their female counterparts, are many of the moths. For example, the giant silk moth males have elaborate and large featherlike antennae that resemble a pair of plumes. Their enlarged feathery ornamentation offers much more than visual appeal. These elaborate plumes are specially designed and equipped to detect the tiniest amounts of female sex pheromones, aiding the male in

"THE DREAM OF ALL ♂ SILK MOTHS" LARGER THAN LIFE ANTENNAE! "YES!"

Giant male silk moth

locating and selecting a proper mate. Since the female is the attractant and perfume source, she has no need for such hi-tech receiving equipment and her antennae are much simpler in design.

Mosquitoes and midges have similar sharp differences in antennae design, but the fuzzier antennae of the male midge and mosquito are equipped to detect the distinct vibrating sounds of flying females. The buzzing that we hear as a female mosquito flies about our head is certainly annoying, but the same sound is a beautiful love call to the male mosquito, as the vibrations of her flight tickle his fancy antennal sensors. The Beach Boys' lyrics "I'm picking up good vibrations" could be the sexual theme song for the mosquito.

Antennae are not the only head paraphernalia that may differ between sexes. The males of swarming flies and midges often have eye facets greatly enlarged near the tops of their heads. Male dragonflies have heads that are almost completely covered by eye facets. In both cases, the expanded eyes on males offer advantage in locating mates. Big-eyed males versus smaller-eyed females are the rule, giving new meaning to the wolf's answer to Little Red Riding Hood: "the better to see you with."

In the insect sex-difference category, many contestants would stand out for their different bodies and colors. It is often the case that female insects are significantly larger than males of the same species. Some male walkingsticks, for example, seem dwarfed by their female mates, and when sexually engaged it looks like the male is a youth along for a ride.

As is typical with many species of birds, insect sexes may be separated by their distinctly different colors and color patterns, especially among the butterflies. Some butterfly males and females are so different in color and design that you would think they were completely different species. Fortunately for those butterflies, the males and females do not get confused. A principal reason for lack of confusion among the butterfly sexes is the distinctive perfume the female of each species emits. The sources of these perfumes are often noticeable structures that distinguish the sexes. Some have specialized hairs that give off the odor, which may be aggregated into "hair pencils," special groups of hairs that serve as scent-producing organs.

Hair pencils for sex, not writing

Some hair pencils form very obvious ornaments on the tip of the female butterfly's body, making a comparison of the sexes easy. In this case, the female could say "I'll show you mine," but the male wouldn't have anything comparable to show in return.

Another very noticeable sex difference occurs in several wasps. There is one wasp, called the velvet ant, whose female lacks wings and is flightless. She is somewhat antlike in appearance and is covered in thick, brightly colored, velvety hair, usually red or orange—the insect punk look. The male is basically bald all over, lacking any velvety appearance, and he possesses four wings and is a good flier. The other big difference, that any

Velvet ant, a wasp in disguise

careless person will quickly discover, is that the female has a sting and the male does not.

Try to pick up a velvet ant female and she will deliver one or several painful stings. For wasps and bees, the stinger is actually a modified egg laying device. Hence, only females are so equipped and only females can threaten with a sting.

Among insects known as the leaf-footed bugs, males show off large ornaments on their hind legs. The hind legs of some males are enlarged and flattened, resembling leaves. The leaflike legs may be quite colorful and they may also be fully

BETS ARE ON !

Leaf-footed bugs locked in combat

adorned with spines and spikes. Such conspicuous males defend territories and compete for mates, frequently getting into "I'll show you mine" contests. Some leaf-footed bugs go beyond showing off their legs and instead use their enlarged legs to fight rival males (Mitchell 1980). Just as in arm wrestling, male bugs lock enlarged hind legs and engage in contests of strength.

So, the insect response to the challenge, "Show me yours and I'll show you mine" gets awfully complicated. It would be helpful to specify in advance exactly what sex part or accessory you want to compare: genitals, horns, jaws, pincers, antennae, eyes, body, color, wings, or legs.

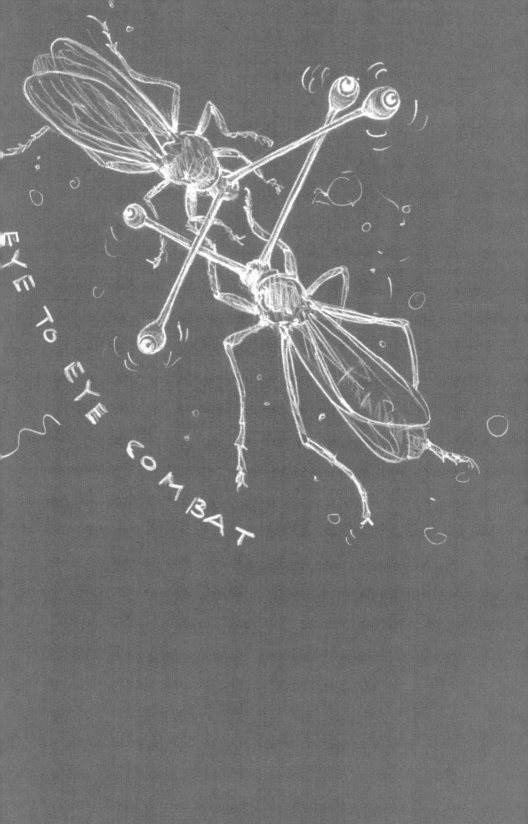

10

The Well-Endowed Male

EYE TO EYE COMBAT

Author's note: So that you don't begin to think that I have some unusual preoccupation with insect genitals and wish to perversely dwell on sexual anatomy, you should be aware that the study of insect genitalia is a significant and highly legitimate area of scientific research. Countless journal articles are written on the evolution, structure, and function of insect genitalia, complete with detailed illustrations and electron microscope photographs of every part. The topic is so important that an entire book has been written on

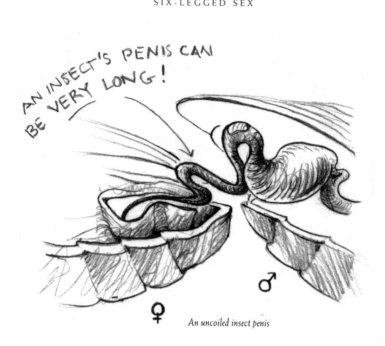

An uncoiled insect penis

the genitalia of a single family of flies, the Bombyliidae, and one can peruse a glossary of genitalia in insects in Taxonomist's Glossary of Genitalia in Insects.

There may be different interpretations of what "well-endowed" means when it comes to insects. Some males (see Chapter 11) are well-endowed in terms of fancy design and specialized function. The penis may have dual functions, for efficiently delivering its own sperm and for eliminating that of competitors. But there are other special endowments for the insect male, both in design and in size.

Bigger and Better

Many male insects (mayflies, cockroaches, mantids, and earwigs) are blessed with some kind of paired or forked penis design (Scudder 1971). The specific style varies among these insects, but each has adopted the strategy that two is better than one.

There are also varied endowments for structures designed to stimulate the female, and for sensitive male structures to be stimulated when in contact with female parts. These are primarily microscopic hairs that presumably tickle or get tickled during sex, providing the stimulation required by both male and female. Many males have "claspers" associated with the penis, which aid the mating pair in staying together during the sex act. The insect penis comes in elaborate designs with variations in special spines, inflatable structures, and interlocking devices that prevent other sexually greedy males from a copulatory coup d'etat. Some caddisflies even have additional paired clasperlike structures called *titillators* (Scudder 1971), a name that implies there's more than clasping going on. To be a well-endowed male literally takes on new and unbelievable proportions when it comes to certain true bugs, beetles, flies, and fleas. Some of these insects are known for exceptionally long sex organs. One picture-winged fly has the ultimate bragging rights when it comes to sheer size (Thornhill & Alcock 1983). It has a coiled penis that when fully extended equals the length of the fly's body! This must surely be the world record holder for relative length, not just within the world of insects, but throughout the entire animal kingdom. At least one would hope so. Organs of comparable length in large land animals would be somewhat frightening.

Look at the Eyes on That Guy!

The male insect may be sexually well-endowed, so to speak, in other ways too. The mostly tropical stalk-eyed flies, discussed by Wilkinson and Dodson (1997), are one fine example. These peculiar looking flies have their eyes perched on amazingly long, sideways projecting stalks, some with combined lengths nearly as long as the entire insect body. The male endowed with the longest eyestalks has the appearance of having a wider head, and hence being a larger fly stud. Female stalk-eyed flies prefer the bigger studs. Males can be seen facing off, head to head, comparing the lengths of their eye-stalks and butting heads as part of ritual pre-mating behavior, not too different from jousting male deer, elk, and bighorn sheep. These fly jousts take place on the female's preferred egg-laying grounds. The male winner, usually the most well endowed, then guards the egg-laying site until a female appears. However, he prevents her from entering her favored egg-laying territory until she yields to his sexual advances. She is permitted to lay her eggs, fertilized from a previous mating, only if she allows the new male to mate too. The females have several sexual partners over their lives, but most male partners have achieved that advantage by virtue of their well-endowed head ornaments.

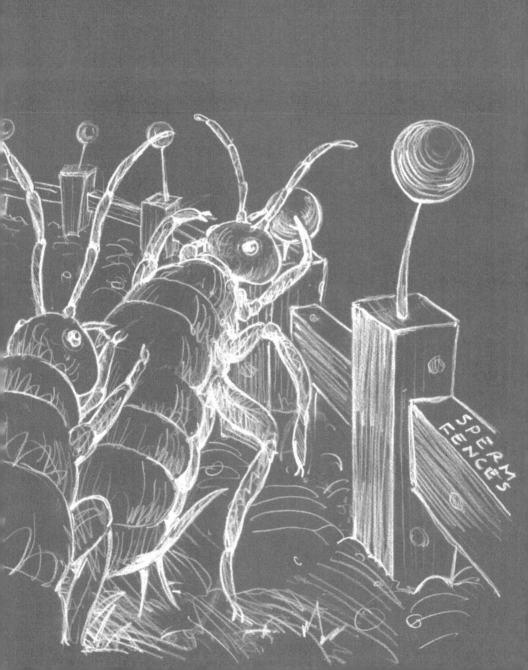

11

My Sperm Are Better
Than Your Sperm

It *may not be surprising to learn that insects compete with each other for sexual partners, as do other animal species. But this competition extends itself to what some would think the extremely bizarre— competing insect sperm. Such competition is not bizarre at all, because the ultimate winner of a mating contest is not necessarily the male that gets to have sex, but the male whose sperm wins the competition to fertilize the egg(s).*

There are many ways that the sperm of one insect can outcompete the sperm from another insect, including being bigger than others, having a cooler design, and being associated with bully behavior.

My Sperm Are Bigger Than Your Sperm

If size counts, give the grand prize to a tiny (a millimeter or less) male feather-winged beetle, whose sperm are up to two-thirds the length of the beetle himself. The gigantic sperm are so large that they literally fill up the female's reproductive system, leaving no room for others. Mated females have been found with sperm tails protruding from their vaginas, the competing sperm unable to enter, completely due to the male feather-winged beetle's giant-sperm blockade (Thornhill and Alcock 1983).

My Sperm Look Cooler Than Your Sperm

If size doesn't matter, then consider fancy designs. Insect sperm come in varied shapes and with magnificent accessories. Some insects have sperm equipped with special enzyme-filled caps that help penetrate the egg. Many insect sperm are powerfully propelled by not just one tail but multiple tails in order to outswim competitors to the egg. Some grasshoppers have sperm armed with barbs so as to create a tangled and not easily displaced

Sperm in all shapes and sizes

roadblock of sperm, blocking the passage of sperm of some inferior design. And if these design strategies were not enough, many insects employ the strategy of overwhelming numbers, flooding the system with countless, fast-swimming sperm (Thornhill and Alcock 1983).

Move Over, Buddy

If none of the above does the trick, then insects resort to overtly bullying behaviors. The supreme sexual bully in the sperm competition game is a damselfly, *Calopteryx maculata*, who has bragging rites for the sexiest penis. His penis is specially equipped for a dual purpose: one, to deliver his sperm to his beloved, and two, to scoop out the sperm that may have been an earlier gift from a competing male. His penis is armed with special hairs and horns (giving new meaning to being horny) for sweeping away any previous sperm deposits. His penis works somewhat like a rotary plumbing device, reaming out the female's sexual pipes to insure they are free of competing sperm. And once the plumbing is cleaned, he fertilizes the female with his own sperm (Waage 1979).

THE INSECT PIPE-CLEANER

PLUMBING DEVICE

Damselfly

Other insects may use similar techniques known as "last in, first out" strategies. For females that have multiple matings with multiple partners, the last male to mate may use his penis to push the competing sperm back into some recess of her system, and then deposit his sperm in a preferred location to insure first fertilization of the eggs. Others may simply flush the female's system with their own ejaculate, leaving her filled with a majority of their own sperm (Thornhill and Alcock 1983).

Watch Your Step

Sperm competition can get even more dangerous outside of the body. Many male insects and insect relatives deposit their sperm as little packets that are then placed on the ground or on some other object for the female to find and pick up. One insect relative, known as the pseudoscorpion (a tiny and harmless scorpionlike creature), will guard the area of ground where it has placed its sperm packets. If it happens upon the sperm packets of another, it will trample and crush them, eliminating some of the competition for females in search of sperm (Proctor 1998).

Right This Way, Miss

The minute male springtail, a six-legged insect relative, is another creature that prefers to place his sperm on the ground. Some actually tend "sperm fields," where a male deposits droplets of sperm called *spermatophores* (Lloyd 1983). He monitors the field, eating older sperm droplets and replacing them with fresh ones, to ensure the highest quality sperm for the female that wanders upon his property. Some males search for females carrying ripe eggs and then place a fence of sperm droplets near her. The male will then push the female toward the fence to achieve the final step of fertilization. Another springtail male leaves less to chance by constructing a spermatophore fence around a target female, so when she steps across the fence—Bingo!—she's fertilized.

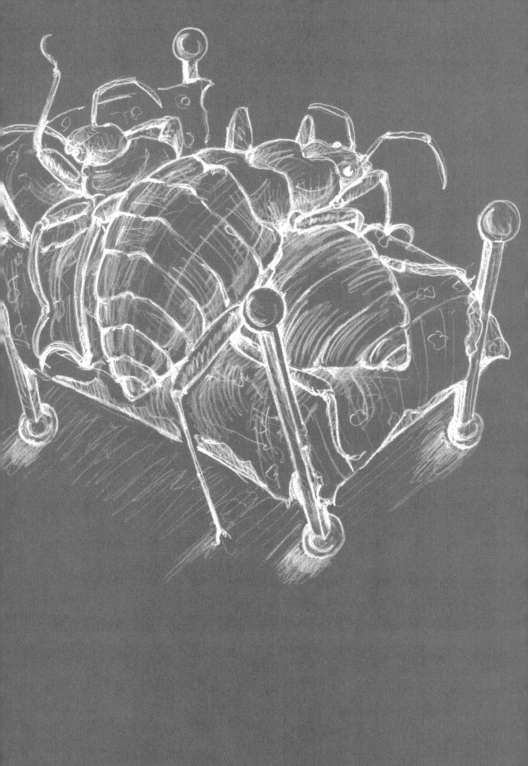

12

Ouch! Watch Where You're Sticking That!

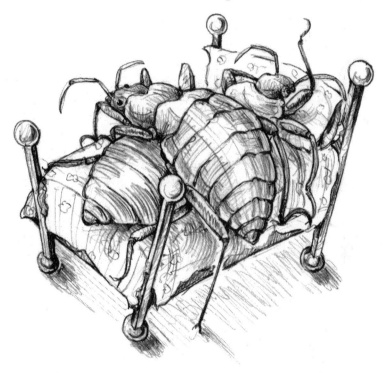

*W*hen it comes to mating, the male bed bug may be the most indelicate of all insects. It is uncouth indeed, and perhaps lazy, or at least guilty of taking the most drastic of sexual shortcuts. There would seem to be no good excuse for its unsavory habits, insofar as both male and female possess the necessary sex organs and systems to allow for a more conventional sex act.

The female, for example, possesses the typical reproductive organs and system of other respectable insects. She has a pair of ovaries for producing eggs, the ductwork to deliver eggs to the outside, and a perfectly nice vagina to accommodate a perfectly nice penis for mating. The male also has the requisite organs and system to accommodate the female; however, the manner in which he employs his penis is where he may be labeled a sexual deviate.

Stabbed for Sex

Rather than inserting his penis into the vagina of his mate, as any respectable male might do, the male bed bug bypasses the conventional route. He stabs the female's body with his penis, poking through the body wall to ejaculate his sperm into her body cavity or into other tissues and organs modified for receiving the sperm. Such an extraordinary act requires an extraordinary penis. Some have described the bed bug penis as a "veritable Swiss army knife of gadgetry" to cut through the female's tissues (Thornhill & Alcock 1983). It is modified like a dagger or knife to penetrate the female's body. Some related bugs with similar sexual habits have a huge, bulky penis that is designed to cut through the vagina and the body cavity to deposit sperm directly in the female's sperm storage organ (Thornhill & Alcock 1983).

Females are not without their own special equipment and design. Some female bed bugs have a special Organ of Berlese to protect against damage due to "traumatic insemination" by males and have no external opening to the vagina (Berenbaum 1995). Furthermore, they have devised a way to digest much of the semen that has found its way into the body. In some bed bugs, sperm actually find their way to the heart, where they accumulate and eventually get distributed with blood to the sex organs or digested along the way (Chapman 1998).

If being stabbed for sex were not bad enough, the injury is followed by the insult of scars on the female body. In some bed bugs, you can determine the number of matings by counting the healed penis wounds on the female's body. Such a scar must be the insect equivalent of the Scarlet Letter.

13

Pardon Me!
I Thought You Were My Wife

*P*lants sometimes become involved in the sex lives of insects, not for the sake of insect satisfaction but rather for their own self-serving interests. One such plant in Australia has co-evolved with an unusual nonstinging wasp species, known to scientists as a tiphiid wasp. To understand the trickery of the plant, one must appreciate the habits and appearance of the insect that it deceives.

The two sexes of the duped wasp species are quite different in appearance, and their courtship and mating habits are directly related to their different forms. Much like the velvet ants described in Chapter 9, female wasps are wingless, and, by the average observer, might be confused with a large ant. The males are more typically wasplike. They are fully winged and narrow-waisted, and they have the other standard characteristics that we associate with being a wasp. The traditional courtship and mating that takes place on the wing in many wasps can't occur with this species because only males can fly. Therefore, the virgin female does the next best thing to flying high: she climbs to a prominent point on some plant, gaining an excellent vantage point for flying insects in the area, and sends out a powerful perfume (pheromone) to lure the sex-seeking male and potential mate. Her pheromone is a strong aphrodisiac, and the combination of sexy odor and the sight of a wingless virgin displaying herself high on some plant are more temptation than any sex-starved male can endure. The closest male flies to her for a sexual embrace. The winged male literally sweeps her off her feet and copulates with the wingless female in frenzied flight.

Insect–Plant Ménage à Trois

The tale of sex for these wasps is complicated by the fact that most males emerge earlier than females; that is, their metamorphosis from pupa to reproductive adult occurs a week or so in advance of the females' metamorphosis. Hence, there are a lot of males in search of females before females come onto the scene. Here's where deceptive plants enter the mating game.

One orchid with a very peculiar-looking flower takes part in an insect–plant ménage à trois. Unlike most orchids, which we think of as having large and beautifully showy flowers, this orchid has a flower that is quite small and not particularly colorful. Nor would it

seem to have an attractive form or
smell, unless you were a male
tiphiid wasp. The flower closely
mimics the appearance of the
female wasp. It is the correct size,
shape, and of similar color, and
it grows on a long stalk at a
height where female wasps could
typically be found luring their mates.

*Sex can be
confusing for
a tiphiid wasp*

Importantly, its odor also mimics the female wasp's
sex pheromone. If the visual mimicry is not perfect, then the
deceptive bouquet adds the final and necessary alluring quality for
the male wasps. Males are attracted to the flowers and fooled to
such an extent that they actually grab the flower and attempt to fly
off with it, still confusing it with a virgin female insect.

The wasp's state of confusion lasts long enough for the flower
to accomplish its purpose: to get pollinated. While attempting to
fly off and to mate with the floral mimic, the wasp inadvertently
gets dusted with the orchid's pollen. From wasps already dusted
with pollen of other orchids, following similar frustrating sexual
acts, the pollen from one flower may transfer to other flowers.

Sexual frustration is greatest for the male wasp that is so duped
by the flower mimic that it attempts to copulate with the flower
(a behavior known as *pseudocopulation*) and actually ejaculates,
condemning its viable sperm to death on the orchid.

But nature is not so cruel as to prevent male wasps from ever
achieving sexual satisfaction. In time, virgin females emerge onto
the scene and the visual and odoriferous lures are dominated by
bona fide female wasps rather than by their floral mimics, most of
which have been successfully pollinated and whose flowers have
withered away. Nature's plan is to use the sexy male wasps first for
servicing orchids, and second for servicing their own kind.

14

Sexual Stamina

Most insects may not impress us with their sexual stamina, whether it be measured by duration of the sex act or their ability to repeat the act over and over again. But what should impress us is that insects have proven their ability as sexual creatures by populating virtually every corner of the earth, and in numbers that are exceeded only by microorganisms such as bacteria. By this measure, the insects have demonstrated the ultimate in sexual stamina, reproducing more of their kind than all other animal and plant species combined, for millions of years. Total populations aside, there are still some impressive record-holders when it comes to insect sexual stamina.

How Long Do They Do It?

To appreciate the champion in the sex-act duration category, compare some average times. Most insect sex acts can take place over a few minutes to a few hours. For instance, among thirteen fly species whose staying powers were summarized by Thornhill and Alcock (1983), there are a couple of fruit flies that copulate anywhere from thirty seconds to ninety minutes, and several other flies that get their sexual business done within an hour. There are some other kinds of fruit flies and flesh flies that can go on as long as three to four hours.

The fly on this list that holds what some might say is the unenviable record of quickest in sex is a type of midge that completes the deed in three to five seconds. At the other end of the spectrum is the championship category, greatest sexual athletes in long distance (by time) events. The lovebug, another type of midge, can help restore the sexual pride of all midge fans with its personal record of over fifty hours. Under scientific laboratory observation, the equivalent of a Masters and Johnson sex study, the lovebug's sex act lasted fifty-six hours. They are clearly not inhibited by scientists who like to watch, and it's easy to see how this midge earned the name lovebug.

But records, as they say, are made to be broken, and the lovebug is no longer first in its category. Another insect called the soapberry bug, a member of an insect group labeled the true bugs, is the current record holder. Mated bugs remain in each other's sexual embrace for up to eleven days! That exceeds the entire adult life span of many insects.

How Often Do They Do It?

The other way to evaluate insect sexual stamina is by the frequency of sex. There are countless examples of insect species that mate with multiple partners or mate multiple times with a single partner. Crickets are among those most often cited for repetitive sex, but perhaps we should give credit to the mountain pine beetle for its honeymoon performance.

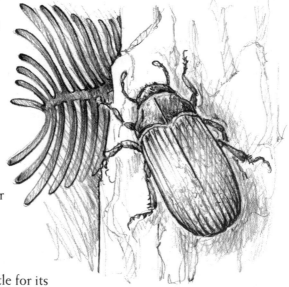

Mountain pine beetle sex awaits under bark

The mountain pine beetle, like other species of bark beetles, invades forests in search of vulnerable trees, often those damaged or weakened by fire, disease, injury, or age. Adult beetles bore through the bark and set up nuptial galleries in the nutrient-rich tissue just beneath the bark. Males are attracted to the females, who are busy tunneling beneath the bark, constructing galleries and readying for family life. The male is attracted by the strong pheromones released while she is engaged in what equates with nesting behavior. The copulations between newlywed bark beetles can be quite rough on the first day of the honeymoon and they occur repeatedly. By day two, the wild pair slows down a bit, and the frequency of sex may taper off to once a day, like the dosage of a good multivitamin supplement. Eventually the female begins depositing her eggs in the nuptial gallery and the honeymoon comes to an end.

15

The Sexually Inhibited Insect

HEADLESSLY IN LOVE!!!

N*early half a century ago, a famous insect physiologist named K. D. Roeder wrote about the peculiar sexual inhibitions and behavior of the praying mantid (Roeder 1953). Roeder's research and other reports, according to Berenbaum (1999), may have given rise to twisted facts and exaggerations in the scientific literature about mantid sexual behavior and cannibalism. As Berenbaum (1999) states, "People hate to let go of things sick and twisted . . ." Perhaps some folklore has been established around mantid sex and some or all of the "facts" need to be re-examined. The following documents what may be a mix of scientific fact and popular science folklore.*

The praying mantid is an insect familiar to many and it is often perceived as an insect with a voracious appetite. Its reputation is well deserved because it is among the best examples of insect predators. The mantid is a formidable insect carnivore, with large and powerful front legs, armed with spines, to reach out, grasp, and firmly hold struggling prey. Its vision is excellent. Thanks to its bulging eyes and swivel-like neck, the mantid is alert to the most subtle movement in its vicinity. Its quick reflexes and strong jaws are more than adequate for devouring a wide range of hapless insects and other small animals. In dinosaur terms, it may be fairly called the T. Rex of insects.

Caution: Dangerous Sex Ahead

The mantid's sexual appetite is also strong, but sometimes the appetite for food and the appetite for sex become intertwined. An interpretation of Roeder's account suggests that male mantids are not sexually inhibited when they begin to search for females, but searching for and stalking females may be a fatal attraction. The female is no less a predator than the male, and she is not above making a meal of her potential mate. Consequently the male mantid, at first sight of a female, freezes in his tracks so as not to catch the attention of the ever-hungry female and risk an attack. Cautiously he begins to stalk the female, sometimes taking over an hour to travel just one foot in distance. This is insect tiptoeing at its best. But with one false move the female may strike, decapitating the male, and proceeding to dine on his head, mantid brain and all.

Headless Sex

One would think that a headless mantid has lost not only his life but certainly his sexual desire. But *au contraire*, for the brain of the male mantid is actually a source of neurotic sexual inhibitions. Losing his brain causes his body to immediately make violent copulating movements, movements that were inhibited by the intact brain nerve signals. It's as if the abdomen and entire sexual apparatus is always in the "on" position, body ready to copulate, but held in check by the brain that continuously sends signals that act as a stop sign for sex. The headless male mounts the female, abdomen thrusting, and positions himself over the female and achieves sexual penetration. A generous donation of sperm is made by the decapitated body, while the female, paying no regard to the valuable gift-giving, casually eats her husband. Eating her husband, presumably, turns out to be a good thing for her offspring because his digested body parts are very nutritious for the developing eggs.

The male need not be sacrificed for a successful mating. The lucky or most cautious male does not disturb the female and hops atop her before she attacks. It seems that once she is in the male's embrace her instinct to attack is somewhat inhibited and the male's sexual inhibitions are temporarily lost. With head and brain intact, he is able to copulate. It is still risky business, and if for some reason the male should not perform, the female need only rotate around a bit to bite off his head and trigger the body to do what comes naturally.

Indeed, sex and cannibalism may be the exception rather than the rule, something that occurs in an artificial laboratory setting, but not in nature (Berenbaum 1999). But even if the behavior is an unnatural artifact of being in a laboratory, the praying mantid gives new meaning to the cliché "losing one's head over love."

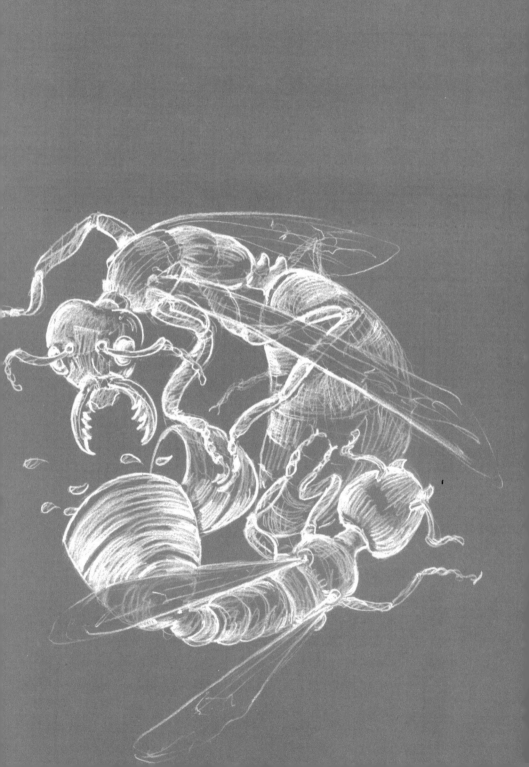

16

Insect Chastity Belts

As with many human inventions, insects were way ahead of us. The British may be credited with bringing notoriety to the chastity belt when, during the Crusades, soldiers left their women adorned with the dreadful device so their ladies' chastity could be preserved until the soldiers' homecoming. But insects had been using chastity belts for millions of years prior to the Crusades and deserve the patent. Furthermore, the insect chastity belt comes in a variety of imaginative styles, with far greater utility than the ugly and cumbersome metal devices used by humans.

Homemade Devices

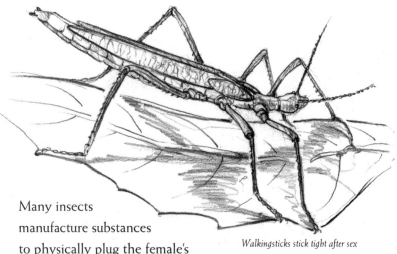

Walkingsticks stick tight after sex

Many insects manufacture substances to physically plug the female's genital opening, thus establishing an effective barrier, or at least what seems like an annoying impediment, to the next male attempting to have sex with the female. Many butterflies, honey bee drones, and some midges place mucus, or some other substance that coagulates or hardens, inside the female. Other butterflies and certain beetles accomplish the same goal by placing an external plug on the female's genital opening. Internal or external, the result is the same. The male's homemade chastity belt guards his mate against other males.

Sometimes these mating plugs are short-lived. Some may dissolve, and the chastity belts in certain mosquitoes are gone in 24 hours, as is potentially the chastity of the females.

The male walkingstick overcomes the dissolving plug problem and provides a little extra insurance against unwanted matings by acting as a "living chastity belt" (Alcock & Thornhill 1983). The much smaller male simply remains coupled with his mate for a long period after the sex act, his body and sex organs blocking the way for other potentially interested males.

Mutilations and Suicide

Sacrificing one's body as a chastity belt goes to the extreme in the suicidal and self-mutilating acts of some biting midges (Ceratopogonidae) and drone honeybees. These males leave their severed sex organs behind, intact in the females' bodies, when they disengage from sex and attempt to fly away. The tightly fitting severed penis serves as a perfect chastity belt.

Sometimes the sacrifice of one's special body parts does not appear voluntary. There are examples of female assault and battery on males for the acquisition of chastity belts. Some harvester ant females, wishing to disengage from their sexual partners, will bite at the male's abdomen, causing him to separate and to leave his penis and a substantial part of his body behind. The severed body, with all of its sexual accessories, remains in place and serves as another weird variety of chastity belt.

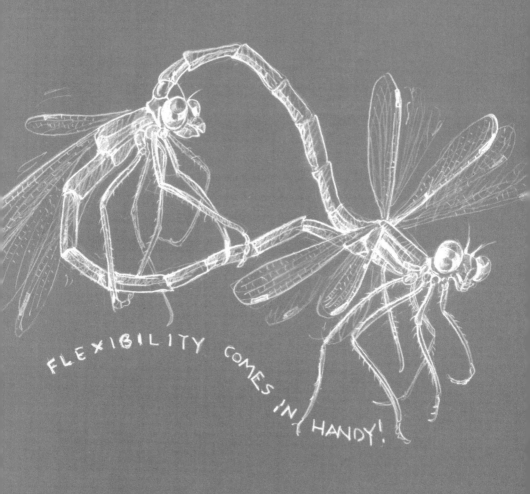

FLEXIBILITY COMES IN HANDY!

17

The Insect Kama Sutra and Other Sexual Acrobatics

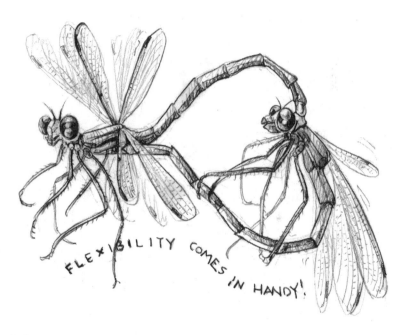

FLEXIBILITY COMES IN HANDY!

The "missionary position" is only one of several sexual postures preferred by insects. Many alternative positions would impress an expert contortionist. Some coupled males twist their organs and bodies from 180 to 360 degrees. Probably the most familiar insect mating position is like that seen in ladybird beetles, with the male riding on top of the female, each facing the same direction. Mounted beetles, with their shell-like wing covers, conjure images of mounted turtles and tortoises. Grasshoppers and their relatives may employ similar male-superior positions, but with the male mounted somewhat to the female's side. Some insects abandon the male-superior approach entirely and link up end to end, facing opposite directions, each upright or with one upside down relative to the other. The possibilities among all insects seem limitless when one factors in the bizarre twisting of organs and body parts that occurs for a sexual union.

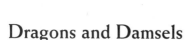

Grasshoppers
preparing to mate

Dragons and Damsels

Certainly among the most contortionistic are the dragonflies and damselflies that mate in the wheel position. A male makes preparations before mating by transferring a loaded sperm packet from the tip of his abdomen, where his primary sex organs are located, to a pouch up front and on the underside of the abdomen. The male is then ready to seek his mate. Once a receptive female is found, the male uses special sex-clamps on the rear of his abdomen to grab the female behind her head, while she simultaneously curls her abdomen forward in a circle or wheel-like shape. Her genitalia, located at the tip of her abdomen, then unite with the male's sperm pouch and fertilization can finally take place. It is an effective but roundabout way to have sex and no other insect does it with similar flair.

Mating skippers

Bee Acrobats

Sexual acrobatics sometimes involve more than mere copulation.

Thornhill and Alcock (1983) discuss an acrobatic male bee that must cling to his mate in flight as she forges from flower to flower during a prolonged mating. An added challenge is the occasional attempt by another male to move in and take over. The sexually engaged male bee, when confronted by such disrespectful peers, flips his body backward, catapulting the interloper away from his mate while managing to maintain his sexual embrace.

Anytime, Anywhere

Just to spice things up a bit, insects with their diverse sexual positions and acrobatics, can be found having sex at any place, at any time. These copulating creatures may be on the ground, in the air, on plants, underground, under water, on the water, and even in their food. Some, like dung beetles, prefer sex in fresh manure and others, like carrion beetles, copulate in carcasses. Lice and fleas mate "on board" birds, animals, and people. They do it in the daylight and they do it at twilight. They do it all through the night. Most have a preferred season for sexual activity, but worldwide you can bet that some insects somewhere are having intimate relations. They do it often and they do it well, judging by the fact that there are more kinds of insects on the planet than all other animal and plant species combined.

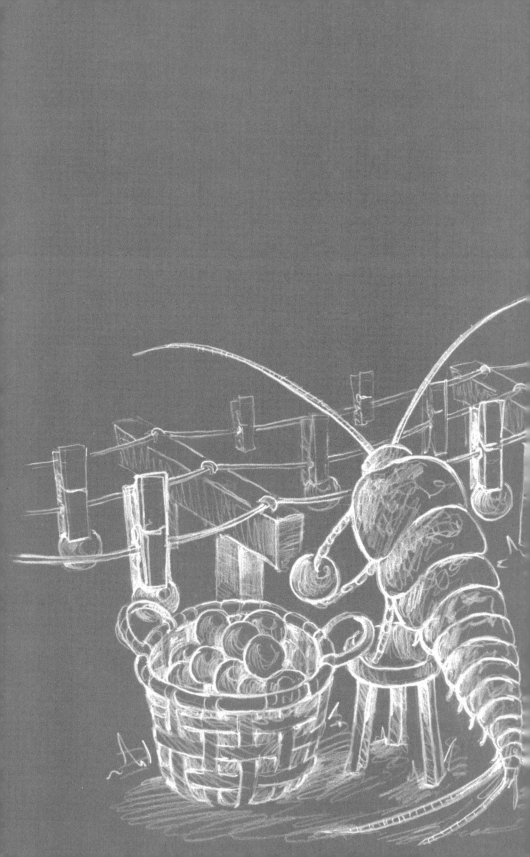

18

Bug Bondage and Insect S & M

One of the most primitive insects, known as the silverfish, seems to have evolved some fairly advanced sexual techniques. Most people know the silverfish as a small, three-tailed, wingless little creature that sometimes becomes a pest in homes, schools, and libraries where it prefers to feed on starchy substances such as fabrics, paper, and books. While we are busy shooing them from our attics and basements or zapping them with insecticides, we are not likely to catch a glimpse of their intimate moments together.

Like the dragonflies and damselflies discussed in the previous chapter, whose males produce packets of sperm that can then be transferred to females outside of the body, the male silverfish also manufactures tiny sperm packets. They are strategically deposited in the favorite hangouts of female silverfish to increase the chances that an unmated female will encounter one and be enticed to latch onto it and then have her eggs fertilized by the viable sperm it contains.

Tie Me Down

The silverfish's habit is reminiscent of "sperm field" production by the minute springtail, discussed in Chapter 11, in which sperm are strategically placed for female retrieval. Not unlike hanging clothes out on the line, male silverfish may deposit their sperm along lines of silk, and the female silverfish uses the silk line as a guide to obtain her sperm (Thornhill and Alcock 1983). Some silverfish males add a bondage step that may increase their odds for successful fertilization. Berenbaum (1995) tells about silverfish males that escort their potential sexual partners to the site where they have left a sperm packet. The male requires no handcuffs, rope, or twine because he is the manufacturer of his own sturdy brand of silk. He ties the female down with his silk, keeping her in bondage until she picks up the treasured package and inserts it in the appropriate body opening.

Do not think for a minute that all insects or spiders that spin silk do so only to spin cocoons or construct webs. The male lynx spider is a good example of eight-legged bondage. The male begins his courtship by stroking the female's back with his front legs. In response, she may walk away or drop from a leaf, dangling from her silken thread. The male will climb down her line and begin to twirl her around, while his silk trails across her body, which has been likened to threading a twirling bobbin (Preston-Mafham 1998). Eventually she becomes well wrapped and he mates with his bound companion.

It seems that such bondage is not too confining because females are often able to escape but usually choose to stay tied for the duration of the sex act. Some, however, will not lie still and remain tied, and once free of the male's silken bonds the female eats him. The European crab spider is another spider that prefers bondage with sex, but it binds its mate loosely to a leaf. The female can easily break free, but she apparently chooses to cooperate and rests motionless during sex.

Toxic Semen

Usually no harm is done with insect and spider bondage, but there are other

Crab spiders enjoy bondage

examples of far more dangerous sexual relations. Sometimes tables are turned and heterosexual sex results in the death of the female and the male is to blame. Some fruit fly males have powerful semen that can have toxic effects. There are certain proteins in the male's semen that can increase female egg laying and simultaneously decrease her sexual appetite. This is to the advantage of the male who mated with her and to the disadvantage of potential male competitors, because his sperm have more eggs to fertilize and his mate is no longer receptive to the sexual advances of others. Another protein in the semen is more toxic, killing off competitor's sperm and inadvertently killing the female fruit fly. Females are not defenseless and, in fact, have their own chemical arsenal within their reproductive ducts to counter the effects of male semen. Chemical warfare may break out inside her system, with sperm winning or losing the battle. In instances where male toxic semen prevails, females die early deaths.

19

Insect Orgies

*A*ccording to Merriam Webster's Collegiate Dictionary, Tenth Edition (*1999*), *an orgy may be "a sexual encounter involving many people; also, an excessive sexual indulgence." I will not be subjective and judgmental by suggesting insects indulge excessively in sex. What may be viewed as excessive by some is clearly serving insect survival. However, it is a matter of scientific fact that by the first definition, insects (substitute for people in* Webster's *definition) participate in sexual encounters involving many insects.*

There are countless examples of "gang sex," multiple males mounting, mating, and attempting to mate with single females. I see it every day in the mealworm colony at work where male beetles clamber atop other male beetles, all attempting to copulate with the same female. Rather than focus on this "ho-hum" type of insect orgy, let's explore the masters of the insect sex orgy—mayflies and true flies.

Sex on the Wing

Mayflies are delicate, winged insects that emerge from watery habitats, primarily rivers and streams, after spending most of their lives feeding as underwater nymphs. In fact, once they emerge as reproductive adults, their lives are nearly at an end because males and females die immediately after their honeymoons, or, more accurately, during their honeymoons. Many do not even eat as adults.

The sole function of the adult mayfly is to mate, and, for the female, to deposit eggs in her former aquatic home. They have literally minutes or hours to accomplish the task, because their life clock is ticking fast once they emerge as flying adults. Therefore, it is extremely critical for mayfly mating success to have a synchronized emergence, a very narrow window of time when the males and females of the same species appear, all with strong sexual appetites. They do so by swarming. Swarms are formed by thousands of flying mayflies, dominated by males, and they position themselves over or near their aquatic habitats like insect clouds. They fly about and seem to bounce, dance, and hover like puppets on a string. Collectively they are easily seen, which is the function of large swarms, and they stand an excellent chance of capturing the attention of newly emerged virgin females (far better, it is presumed, than individually cruising for females). The females are on the lookout for seductive swarms and will fly toward one once it is spotted. The males are no less vigilant. With exceptionally large and specially designed eyes, they watch for approaching virgins, and the most alert male will fly out of the swarm to meet the female in a mayfly embrace. Sex may be confined to the two consenting adults, but develop from the stimulating sexual encounter with a mob of males, sharing a common purpose.

Mayfly sex is perilous. Many mayflies, during adult emergence, are devoured by fish and birds, never making it to the orgy. The orgy itself, or swarm, is a deliciously large target for birds and bats. The mayflies that make it to the honeymoon phase and successfully mate are also doomed. After mating, males typically return to the swarm, but their lives are nearly over. Within hours or a day, they die and drop to the ground or water to be consumed by scavengers, or to rot. Females are short-lived too, dying after the eggs have been deposited, or dying with eggs oozing from the body during their death throes on the water surface. Countless eggs are eaten before they settle to the bottom or before the mayfly nymphs hatch.

Mayfly sex can be perilous to people, too, at least during the orgy phase. Some mayfly swarms and populations are so massive that their dead bodies have covered roads and bridges, piling up as a thick and slippery hazard. Unsuspecting automobile drivers can hit these slippery zones and have an insect-induced crash. The road sign "Slippery When Wet" may need to be changed to "Slick Sex Ahead."

Orgy Landmarks

Many flies share the habit of attending sex orgies, and swarm in a fashion similar to mayflies. Midges and mosquitoes, which are types of flies, are among the best examples. Their swarms are also gangs of sex-seeking males and they too form insect clouds to attract the young virgin midge or mosquito. Their swarms are typically found near water or marshy areas, homesites for their eggs and larvae, and are a common sight for fishermen. Some people find these swarming flies to be quite a nuisance, especially when they seem to accidentally swarm around a person's head and face. But what seems accidental may actually be a purposeful act. Many swarming insects

Swarming flies annoying a human being

use prominent landmarks for orientation. Swarming flies may choose a prominent bush, tree, fence post, or human being to swarm above. The chosen person may swat at the flies or walk away to escape the pesky insects, but often to no avail as the swarm regroups over its newly claimed human landmark. Rather than cursing the nuisance midges, a person may choose to feel flattered and privileged to have been selected by thousands of flies as their sexual landmark.

20

Insect Prostitutes

*P*rostitution may be too harsh a term for the sexual relationships of some insects because insects do not deal in currency. There are, however, many insect sexual transactions in which food is provided as payment, like money. A common example of insects using food as payment is nuptial feeding, the male offering food to females in exchange for sex. A more romantic interpretation of such behavior could be likened to a Valentine's Day gift of chocolate, as discussed in Chapter 5. Whether it's prostituting themselves for food or *taking advantage of nuptial gifts for some survival and evolutionary advantage, certain male and female insects engage in sex for favors.*

As noted in Chapter 6, some male insects entice females to mate by offering nutritious packages of semen. These nuptial gifts come in a variety of forms, in a variety of insects. Certain katydid males produce a large sperm packet full of nutrients that is highly prized by females. The katydid's "glandular gift" (Gwynne 1997) is eaten by the female, seemingly as payment for sex, but the benefits from the supplemental nutrition include greater egg production and higher survivorship for her offspring.

No Food, No Gift, No Sex

Another variation on the glandular secretion theme is found among certain cockroaches, fruit flies, beetles, and the scorpionflies. One of these male scorpionflies, so named because some males have tails resembling a true scorpion, will find and feed upon a dead insect, producing a large amount of salivary juice. He will deposit this juice in a sizeable mound on the ground and guard it, while luring a receptive female with his strong sex cologne or pheromone. The attracted female eats the juicy pile and, in return for the male's investment of time and energy, there is an agreeable copulation.

Females may be quite choosy when it comes to selecting and receiving nuptial food and gifts. Some male dance flies, for example, capture insect prey and display their individual gifts while swarming in large groups with other gift-bearing males. Some males may have captured large and tasty prey, while others may have been less successful and have less-appealing nuptial gifts to offer. Discriminating females fly into these male swarms and shop around, size up the gifts, and eventually select a male with the largest prey. She may still not be prepared to offer sex until she examines the prey offering further and tastes it to see if it is really to her liking. If not, she'll leave the male's embrace before sexual intimacy, and seek another male who has more to offer.

Other scorpionflies are quite notorious for their manner of sexual gift giving. First, males will acquire dead insects through their own collecting, or they may steal from other males. Some are so brave as to steal dead insects from dangerous spiderwebs. The male then guards his gift while calling to potential mates with his cologne. One group, called the hanging scorpionflies, does so while hanging from branches with their front legs and prominently displaying

Hanging scorpionflies

their gifts with their hind legs. The powerful sex pheromone is released from large glands on the abdomen. The combined scent and visual display excites females who fly toward the male and grab onto the prey. While clinging to the dead prey and eating her nuptial gift, the two may copulate—if the gift is satisfying to the female. Once again, females are selective, and if the prey is too small or if she does not like its taste, she will resist the male's seductive advances by either interrupting the sexual act or not permitting him to begin. There is a definite advantage to providing good payment; the larger the gift, the longer the time for copulation.

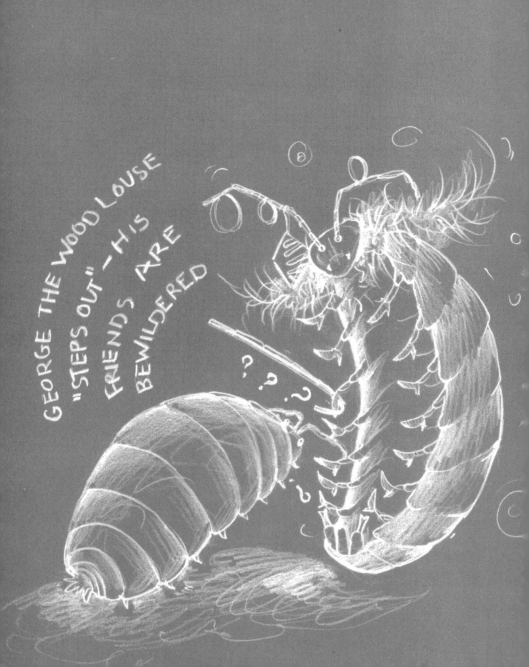

21

Insect STDs

It appears that the insect world is not immune or protected against sexually transmitted disease. However, insect STDs do not include the well-known culprits: gonorrhea and syphilis caused by bacterial infection, and viral-caused Herpes and AIDS. But rather, in every major insect group (known as insect Orders) there is potential for infection by another kind of sexually transmitted bacterium called Wolbachia. Wolbachia does something more interesting and bizarre than simply causing a disease: it controls the insect's sex life.

The Paths to Infection

Wolbachia, estimated to be present in 5–10% of all insect species, may only survive in the egg cells of females. The infected females are not harmed, nor do they come down with symptoms as a result of the bacterial infection, but they do sacrifice some of their reproductive rights. *Wolbachia*-infected females are apparently more fit than noninfected individuals, but in exchange for higher fitness comes the obligation to mate only with other *Wolbachia*-infected individuals. The *Wolbachia*-infected female can only successfully mate with a *Wolbachia*-infected male. The *Wolbachia* bacterium in an egg fertilized by a noninfected male will kill the sperm or the union's offspring. The seemingly advantageous strategy of avoiding sex with individuals infected with sexually transmitted bacteria is turned on its head with insects. It has become the best strategy for two infected individuals to become sexual partners.

Unfortunately for the males, they do not make particularly good hosts for the *Wolbachia* bacterium, because they don't have cells that can accommodate *Wolbachia* bacteria as nicely as the female egg cells. Therefore, male insects are something of a dead end for *Wolbachia*, and female reproductive strategy is altered. Instead of mating with males, it is believed that *Wolbachia* bacteria cause some species to become parthenogenetic (see Chapter 25). Parthenogenesis, called virgin birth, is reproduction without males. Female eggs need not be fertilized to grow; however, the unfertilized eggs of parthenogenetic females all grow to become female. The insect population is female only. Males do not exist. Males have become superfluous.

Treatments, Cures, and Unusual Results

But there may be hope for the males. Some researchers have found a "cure" for parthenogenesis by using antibiotics. Females treated for their *Wolbachia* infections with antibiotics will begin to lay eggs that may grow to be either male or female. That's where the good news for the males might end. It seems that parthenogenesis has been so successful and around for so long, that when males are artificially reintroduced into the population, via antibiotic treatments, they are impotent. The next logical step is an insect impotency drug treatment.

Another extreme alteration to some male individuals, resulting from the presence of this mysterious bacterium, is an unwanted sex change operation. In the wood louse, an insect-related crustacean, *Wolbachia* causes a feminization phenomenon. Infected males have their sex glands suppressed and are then transformed into females. It seems that by one strategy or another *Wolbachia* is bent upon eliminating the male sex.

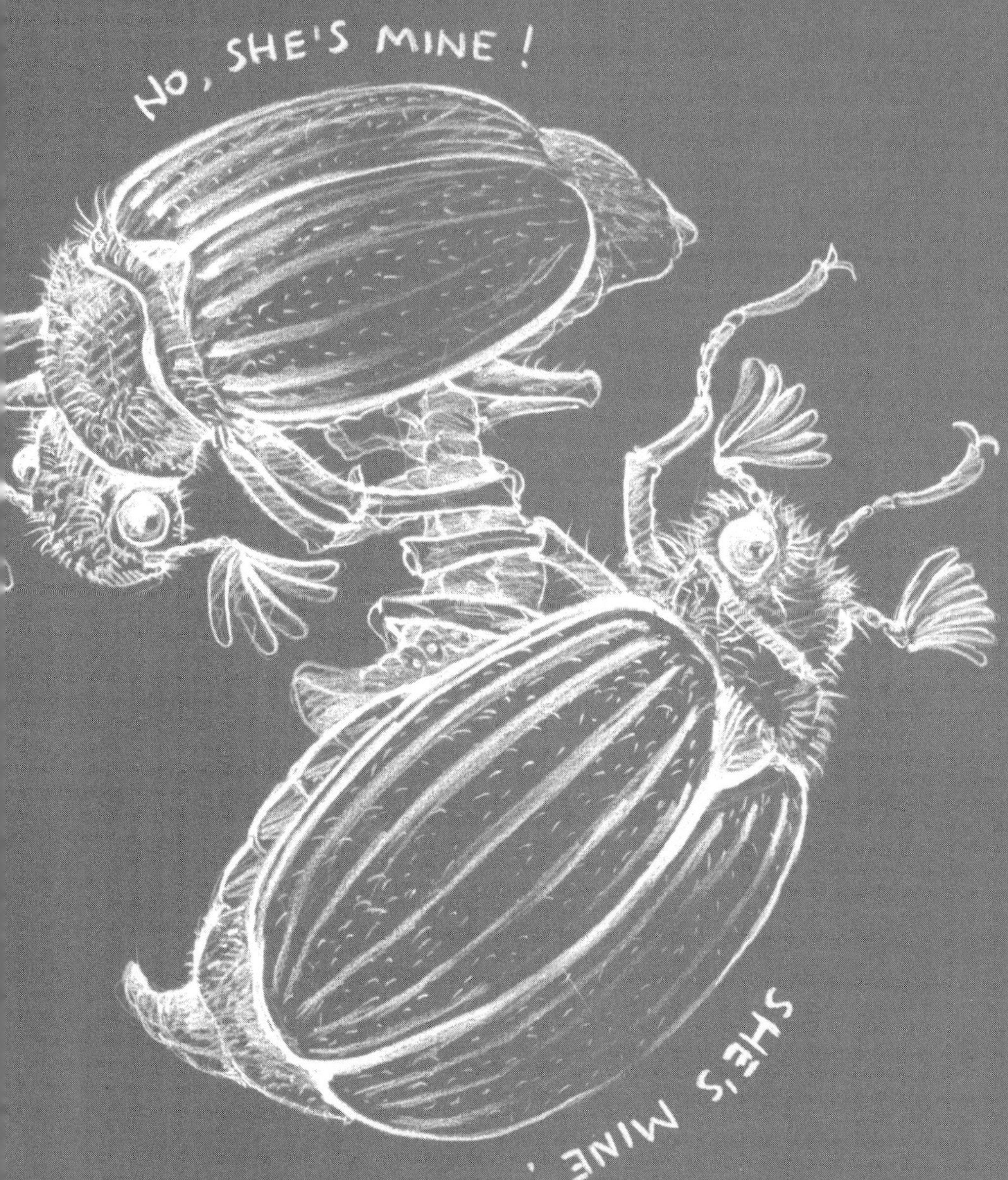
NO, SHE'S MINE!
SHE'S MINE!

22

Insect Sex Crimes

*S*ome insect "criminals and crimes" have already been revealed, such as the murderous femme fatales fireflies (Chapter 3), the fraudulent dance fly (Chapter 5), and the sexual assault by male bed bugs (Chapter 12). But a few other "insect sex crimes" have not yet been mentioned: forced sex, incest, pedophilia, and a crime following sex, infanticide.

Forced Sex

In the insect world there are examples of forced copulations, in which the female choice of mates is compromised. A striking example of such an insect, described by Thornhill and Alcock (1983) as an insect "rapist," is a scorpionfly.

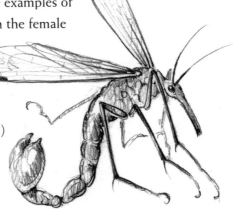

Check out the genital bulb on that scorpionfly

The scorpionfly is a medium-sized insect whose name is derived from the male's superficial resemblance to a scorpion. His abdomen is a bit elongated with an upturned tail that possesses an enlarged genital bulb at the tip, giving him standing among the well-endowed insect males. The untrained person might mistake the genital bulb for a stinger, like that of a true scorpion.

Most scorpionflies are not forceful and overpowering during the sex act. In fact, many are quite cordial in courtship, offering nuptial gifts in the form of tasty insect treats to attractive females, which females then exercise their option to pair up with the male that has the most alluring food offer (see Chapter 21). But it seems there is always one in every crowd to give the others a bad name. *Panorpa banksi* is one such scorpionfly. These males are known to forcefully copulate with females without any enticement or offer of a nuptial gift. The male searches for a female and, upon finding a suitable mate, flies at her, grabbing her by her wing or leg with his specialized pincer-like genitals. As she struggles, he maneuvers in such a way as to allow another clamping organ on his body to more securely hold her, permitting him to position his genitals and inseminate her.

The fact that females resist pairing with males that do not offer nuptial gifts and that they physically struggle to escape suggests that these are forced sex acts and not simply aggressive behaviors to assure matings between fit couples. Furthermore, there is scientific evidence that suggests that females inseminated by these forceful males can still somehow prevent successful sperm transfer in half of the matings. The female forced to copulate is able to prevent unwanted pregnancy half of the time.

Incest

The most common example of what might be considered the insect equivalent of incest occurs among the so-called social insects, bringing new meaning to the term. Social insects include ants, termites, bees, and certain wasps that live communally in nests or colonies. They have a caste system and division of labor, whereby every individual has a genetically predetermined role or set of duties to perform for the good of the colony. One of these duties is sex, and only certain males and certain females (sometimes a sole female) are equipped and privileged to do the deed.

Consider the common honey bee's sex life and incestuous habits. There is only one sexually active female to sustain the colony, and she is the queen bee. Once a virgin queen has mated she assumes the role of an egg factory,

A queen's work is never done

producing thousands of eggs over her multi-year lifetime. She has the ability to determine the sex of her offspring as eggs are being deposited because she controls which eggs get fertilized by the sperm she has stored from her multiple matings. Some sperm are held back and others are allowed to fertilize eggs as they travel through her ducts. Fertilized eggs give rise to females, most of which become sexually sterile worker bees; only a few become sexually fertile queens. Unfertilized eggs give rise to sexually fertile male bees or drones. Therefore, drones are fatherless, having developed only from an egg, without the contribution of a drone's sperm. Over time, the hive is populated with tens of thousands of the queen's male and female offspring, mostly workers, far fewer drones, and only under certain circumstances a few potential new queens. Therefore, every bee in the honey bee colony has the same mother. Only females have a father. They are all sisters and brothers.

So where does the incest come in? It occurs when new queen bees are born. Usually new queens appear when a colony is overcrowded. The established queen bee will be stimulated by overcrowding to recruit thousands of her workers to evacuate the hive. Together they fly off as a swarm in search of a better neighborhood, more specifically a suitable shelter where there is room to establish a new colony with more growing room. The bees that are left behind at the hive—many workers and the drones—nurture the birth of new queens so a rightful heir can be had. The first or strongest new queen, a fertile virgin, to emerge in the queenless hive dispatches any rival virgin queens with stings and then assumes her royal duty—to find a suitable mate and repopulate the colony with her own offspring.

Her choices for mates are the drones in her own hive, her older brothers! Her brothers are as eager as she to mate because that is the only useful job they are capable of doing and they get only one chance in a lifetime to do it. Hence the virgin queen, with powerful sex pheromone as a lure, flies from the hive with her alert older brothers in hot pursuit. Theoretically the most persistent and strongest-flying brother bees succeed in catching up with her. They mate, the males die and she returns to the hive. The unsuccessful and sexually unfulfilled brothers eventually return to the hive, their only chance at sex gone, only to be later summarily kicked out of the hive by their sister workers, because the drones have literally outlived their usefulness.

Thus you can see that this incestuous marriage of queen and drone (sister and brother) will yield new female (workers and potential new queens) and male (drones) offspring. Their deceased father was their uncle, and their mother is their aunt. These are the familial relationships after only two generations. I will leave it to the reader with greater expertise in untangling family trees to determine the relations among bees after further generations of incestuous behavior.

Pedophilia

Two scarab beetles, known as the northern and southern masked chafers, have the dubious distinction of being the closest things to insect pedophiles. At least that is one interpretation that might come from studies reported by Haynes and Potter (1995). In fairness to the chafers, however, and like the stories of many other accused criminals, there are extenuating circumstances that should be considered before we assign a guilty verdict to these otherwise law-abiding beetles.

As adults, the male and female chafers rely largely on chemical communication for sexual encounters. Female chafers emit an attractive-smelling pheromone to arouse and lure their male mates. The sex life of the chafers intensifies after dark. At dusk, the

southern chafer males emerge from the soil and pursue the
pheromone trails of females in zigzagging flights. Their sexual
exploits do not seem too deviant, apart from the fact that many
males may attempt to mate with a single female once they have
caught up with her. Nor do the sexual antics of the northern chafer
appear deviant or dysfunctional. By 11 P.M. the southern chafers
have ceased having sex, and females return to the soil for egg
laying. Around midnight male northern chafers emerge from
underground, exercising what some might regard as sexual good
taste. But to scientists it's an effective adaptation to avoid attraction
between two species that share the same pheromone. The northern
chafers commence a similar repertoire of sexual pursuit and matings,
now in the privacy of their own species. Mated northern chafer
females also return to the ground to deposit eggs.

The sexually dysfunctional part of the chafer beetle's behavior
develops because of some confusing signals emitted from the chafer
youth. Young chafers are called larvae or grubs—soft-bodied,
wormlike forms that live underground, feeding on plant roots. They
are the equivalent of an adult butterfly's caterpillar. They are not
sexually mature. In spite of their immature status, they are
sometimes approached for sex by adult southern or northern chafers
because they happen to possess the same chemical attractant given
off by sexually mature females. Usually this does not pose
problems, because the chafer grubs are hidden below ground and
not detected by the males flying above. However, some chafer
grubs come to the surface prematurely, influenced perhaps by a
bacterial disease they have contracted, and then their pheromone is
detectable but indistinguishable from the pheromone of adult
females. Consequently, both male and female larvae become targets
of mistaken adult chafer beetle sexual advances. It is an odd sight
indeed to see a beetle, or more than one beetle at a time,
attempting to copulate with a grub.

If there is to be a punishment for the chafer's crime, it is the fact that the male's preciously brief sex life and opportunity to pass along his genes have been wasted or at least diminished by the time spent attempting to exploit a grub.

Infanticide

There is widespread killing among insects, mostly for food or in self-defense, and sometimes for sex, as with the honey bee virgin queen who assassinates her rivals to claim a mate and the colony. But the killing also includes sexual offspring, which qualifies as infanticide (Halffter 1997). One example is the dung beetle, so-named because the beetle adults live in and feed on animal dung. The females, after mating, lay their eggs in carefully constructed balls of dung that they roll about and eventually bury beneath the soil. Upon hatching, the beetle grub or larva is in "dung beetle heaven," securely housed and surrounded by its favorite substance, animal dung. Despite how disgusting people might think dung beetles are, the female dung beetle is quite a good mother, at least until conditions deteriorate. She stays with her rolled dung balls and dung ball children, guarding the nest. But if conditions get very dry, the mother dung beetle, up until now exhibiting wonderful maternal care, will begin to feed on the dung balls, sometimes to the point of killing her own grubs, sending them to the real dung beetle heaven.

It's a smelly start to a dung beetle's life

23

Sexual Faux Pas

What may have appeared to be the greatest sexual faux pas in insects (male wasps attempting to copulate with orchid flowers, see Chapter 13) pales in comparison to some other sexual blunders documented in the scientific literature. Thornhill and Alcock (1983) have summarized them, and thankfully included several photographs to prove to any possible skeptics that such remarkable behaviors exist.

Sex After Death

Take for example necrophilia among
digger bees. Digger bees, so named
because they dig burrows for nesting
underground, can get quite
confused. As males dig in search
of female mates, they may
sometimes find dead digger
bees instead. Dead or alive, a
digger bee once discovered is
enough to arouse the sex-hungry male.

Digger bees dig up strange bedfellows

He will attempt to mate with his own dearly departed. The male
digger bee may also encounter other male digger bees in his search,
latch on and attempt to mate. He will eventually dismount in search
of the opposite sex, but sometimes not until he has probed with his
penis enough to discover that everything is not quite right.

Mount First, Ask Questions Later

Homosexual male contact is not uncommon in the insect world.
Males of many species have been seen attempting to mate with
other males: crickets, cockroaches, fleas, bed bugs, lacewings,
butterflies, moths, assorted other bugs, flies, midges, bees, and wasps.

It seems that many of the males' sexual confusion and
misadventures can be blamed on their eagerness to find a partner.
Many male insects essentially mount first and ask questions later.
If something is even in the ballpark as far as shape, form, or smell
is concerned, it might be enough to arouse the sex-seeking male.
This can lead to embarrassing and ridiculous sexual encounters with
the wrong species or, worse yet, inanimate objects. The scientific
literature has documented enough of these examples to suggest that

if insects had to pass the equivalent of a motor vehicle eye test before having sex, many would fail. Some should be tested to determine if they can distinguish their own kind from such things as twigs, bananas, aluminum cans, and beer bottles! All of these things have become love objects for different amorous male insects. The sight of a beetle attempting to copulate with a beer bottle is more amusing to the human observer than it is satisfying to the male beetle. The best explanation for such a sexual faux pas is the overzealous sexual desire of the beetle and his poor ability to discriminate shape and size. Even if an object is only a gross approximation or an exaggerated version of the real target of their affection, it may still stimulate some males to proceed with lovemaking.

Insect Dirty Tricks

For several years my colleagues and I have enjoyed demonstrating these behaviors to students in the classroom (with insects, that is). The classic performers that we have used are beetles from mealworm colonies. Using a technique described by Tschinkle, Wilson and Bern (1967), we entice male beetles to attempt copulation with glass rods that are about the diameter of the female beetle's body. The male beetle is not

Get off me! I'm not a beetle.

tricked by the appearance of the glass rod, but rather by the dirty trick we play on him by adding a sexual scent. We dip the glass rod into a little "essence of female beetle," an extract of her body odor, and then get out of the male's way. The female's odor on the stick elicits a strong sexual response. Even in the presence of legitimate virgin female beetles, males will attempt to copulate with the counterfeit glass rods. They are blinded by the scent of a woman.

24

Sex Wanted: Males Need Not Apply

THE FEMALE BABY FACTORY

If insects advertised for sex in the personals section of the classified ads, the heading "Sex Wanted: Males Need Not Apply" might be seen. It would have been submitted by a highly evolved group of insects, a group in which only females exist. Actually, these females would not need to advertise for any sexual partner because they are capable of taking care of their sexual business completely on their own.

Doing It Alone

There are many examples of such insects,
some of the most common being certain
tiny, stingless wasps that parasitize other
insects. Much to the dismay of
chauvinistic males, the male
model is obsolete. There is no such
thing as heterosexual sex. Nor is there
what we would traditionally call
homosexual sex. Instead, sex is a solo
act by a virgin female wasp. The
proper term for the phenomenon
is parthenogenesis, Greek for
"virgin birth."

Parasitic wasp stings lead to virgin birth

The perpetual-virgin females
are able to produce and deposit
viable eggs in or on the bodies of their
hosts (the insects that they parasitize), giving rise to a new
generation of wasps, all of which are females.

Some insects, such as certain aphids, have also opted for
parthenogenesis but seem to have hedged their sexual bets.
For much of the aphid season only females exist and the females
reproduce without any help from males. They continue to produce
only daughters, but by the fall season a generation of sons and
daughters is produced giving rise to old-fashioned heterosexual
relations. The aphid's virgin birth habits resume the very next
spring, and the cycle of alternating exclusively female generations,
followed by a generation of males and females in the fall, continues.

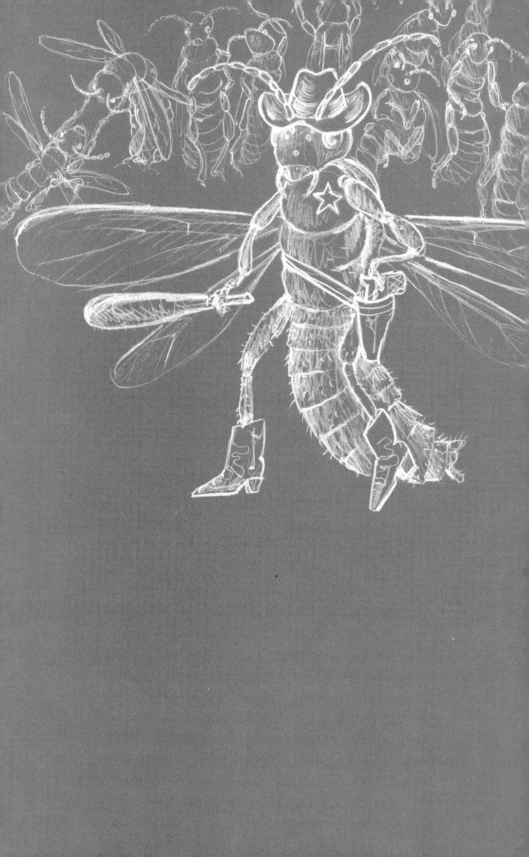

25

Insect Sexual Potpourri

You might think that after devoting twenty-four chapters to the common and bizarre sex lives of insects there would be nothing left to discuss, discover, or imagine; not so with bugs. In fact, we have only begun to touch the surface of six-legged sexual exploits. Furthermore, with literally millions of insects still to be discovered, imagine the delicious opportunities awaiting biologists, entomologists, and insect voyeurs. Countless stories of eroticism remain to be uncovered. This final chapter touches on a few more, including youthful indiscretion, bigamy, and cannibalism. Consider these

*concluding accounts as a small sample
of insect sexual potpourri.*

Precocious Insects—
Babies Having Babies

A tiny gall-midge, *Miastor metraloas,* is
among the sexually precocious. Gall
midges deposit eggs in plant tissues,
which may result in a plant growth,
called a gall, that grows around
the insect, providing a special
shelter and food for the midge.
Most respectable gall midges hatch
from eggs as larvae, which feed and grow

Small midges have a lot of gall

to become pupae, an intermediate step somewhat like a bug
adolescent, before maturing into a sexually reproductive adult.
The precocious *M. metraloas,* however, doesn't wait for adulthood,
or even adolescenthood, to reproduce. The "baby" midge, or larva,
is able to produce viable eggs without male fertilization, and her
eggs develop and grow within her body as her own babies. The
mother larva gives birth to her baby larvae and the cycle can then
repeat itself. Actually the birth is more traumatic for the mother
larva, because the baby larvae consume the mother's tissues and
emerge from her hollowed-out body, a high cost incurred by
babies having babies.

Insect Harems

Long before the establishment of human harems in the Mideast, a
tiny and poorly known insect called a zorapteran could be found in
other tropical and subtropical areas of the world with harems of

their own. The zorapterans are similar in appearance to termites, and are found living in sawdust piles and beneath bark of rotting trees, where they feed on fungi, dead insects, and other small creatures or, in some cases, prey upon the living. Choe (1997) provides an interesting account of some Panamanian zorapterans that keep harems. Zorapteran males compete for mates and a hierarchy of dominant and subdominant males is established in the zorapteran colonies. Dominance is determined in a variety of one-on-one male encounters. Some encounters involve males exhibiting themselves. When males get close to each other, each exhibits his pair of antennae by vibrating them wildly, and the subdominant male may walk away. The encounters can escalate to head-butting contests or rear-to-rear leg-kicking contests, with the strongest male or best kicker declared the dominant male.

The dominant male patrols and guards his harem of females and spends much of his time chasing the females and soliciting sex. The subdominant males are always lurking on the edge of the harem, looking for an opportunity to sneak some sex too. Sometimes they succeed, but the majority of sexual relations happens between the dominant male and the females in his harem.

Cannibal Sex

Finally, excuse for a moment that this book's title is *Six-Legged Sex* and allow me to consider spiders, the eight-legged "cousins" of insects. Among the spiders there are nice examples of "cannibal sex" (Jackson and Pollard 1997). The jumping spider, like other spiders, is a carnivore that feeds upon spiders and insects. As their name implies, they are excellent jumpers, and most opt to stalk and pounce upon their prey, rather than to construct silken webs and lie in ambush. Jackson and Pollard describe one jumping spider that is a web builder, with the very dangerous habit of stalking its prey by entering other spiders' webs. Upon entering another's web, it sends vibrating signals to the resident spider that mimic the vibrations the spider would receive from a struggling insect caught in the web. As the spider approaches what it perceives to be its next meal, the jumping spider pounces on it and literally turns the (dining room) table on the spider. Such aggressive feeding behavior and dangerous tactics in this jumping spider can have dire

Jumping spiders have risky sex

consequences for males when it comes to sex. Jumping spider sex can turn into cannibal sex. A jumping spider female is not averse to eating her own kind. But first there is the obligate courtship, in which both female and male jumping spiders participate. Both beat the spider equivalent of drums by pounding on silk or tugging at it with their legs. Males posture for females by waving legs, vibrating body parts, and walking in exaggerated jerky fashion. Certain female jumping spiders prefer males who dance. Courtship becomes more intimate when the sexes get close as the male provides "love taps" to the female's body. If all goes according to the male's interests, the two will drop from the web in a lover's embrace, suspended by a silken strand.

The female may prefer food to sex, and at any time before or after the act she may quickly turn on her mate and devour him. Therefore, some females elect to take the male's sperm first and dine on him later; others show no interest in getting sperm and simply want to eat. Some females appear to be as deceitful as the males who mimic the vibrations of insects trapped in webs. It seems that the male cannot distinguish immature females from adult females;

hence, if he attempts to court and copulate with a youngster, she will choose nutrition over chastity—another reason why sex should occur only between consenting adults.

Bibliography

Alcock, John. "Postinsemination associations between males and females in insects: the mate-guarding hypothesis." *Annual Review of Entomology*, 39 (1994): 1–21.

Arnqvist, Goren. "The evolution of water strider mating systems: causes and consequences of sexual conflicts." In *The Evolution of Mating Systems in Insects and Arachnids*, edited by J. C. Choe and B. J. Crespi. Cambridge, England: Cambridge University Press, 1997.

Bailey, Winston J. *Acoustic Behaviour of Insects: An Evolutionary Perspective*. London: Chapman and Hall, 1991.

———. and J. Ridsill-Smith, editors. *Reproductive Behaviour of Insects*. London: Chapman and Hall, 1991.

Berenbaum, M. R. *Bugs in the System: Insects and Their Impact on Human Affairs*. Boston: Addison-Wesley, 1995.

———. "A prayer before dining." *American Entomologist*, 45, no. 4 (1999): 195–197.

Borror, D. J., C. A. Triplehorn, and N. F. Johnson. *An Introduction to the Study of Insects*. Philadelphia: Saunders College Publishing, 1989.

Case, J. F. "Vision in mating behaviour of fireflies." In *Insect Communication*, edited by Trevor Lewis. London: Academic Press, 1984.

Catts, E. Paul. "Sex and the bachelor bot." *American Entomologist*, 40, no. 3 (1994): 153–160.

Chapman, R. F. *The Insects: Structure and Function*. Fourth edition. Cambridge: Harvard University Press, 1998.

Choe, J. C. "The evolution of mating systems in the Zoraptera: mating variations and sexual conflicts." In *The Evolution of Mating Systems in Insects and Arachnids,* edited by J. C. Choe and B. J. Crespi. Cambridge, England: Cambridge University Press, 1997.

Choe, J. C., and B. J. Crespi. *The Evolution of Mating Systems in Insects and Arachnids.* Cambridge, England: Cambridge University Press, 1997.

Dafni, A. "Mimicry and deception in pollination." *Annual Review of Ecology and Systematics,* 15 (1984): 259–78.

Daly, H. V., J. T. Doyen, and A. H. Purcell III. *Introduction to Insect Biology and Diversity.* New York: Oxford University Press, 1998.

Edmunds, G. F., Jr., S. L. Jensen, and L. Berner. *The Mayflies of North and Central America.* Minneapolis: University of Minnesota Press, 1976.

Eisner, Thomas, Michael A. Goetz, David E. Hill, Scott R. Smeadley, and Jerrold Meinwald. "Firefly 'femmes fatales' acquire defensive steroids (lucibufagins) from their firefly prey." *Proceedings of the National Academy of Sciences,* 94, no. 18 (1997): 9,723.

Ewing, A. W. "Acoustic signals in insect sexual behaviour." In *Insect Communication,* edited by Trevor Lewis. London: Academic Press, 1984.

Greenfield, M. D. "Sexual selection in resource defense polygyny: lessons from territorial grasshoppers." In *The Evolution of Mating Systems in Insects and Arachnids,* edited by J. C. Choe and B. J. Crespi. Cambridge, England: Cambridge University Press, 1997.

Gwynne, Darryl T. "Glandular gifts." *Scientific American,* 277, no. 2 (1997): 66.

Halffter, G. "Subsocial behavior in Scarabaeinae beetles." In *The Evolution of Social Behavior in Insects and Arachnids,* edited by J. C. Choe and B. J. Crespi. Cambridge, England: Cambridge University Press, 1997.

Hart, Stephen. "When *Wolbachia* invades, insect sex lives get a new spin." *Bioscience* 45, no. 1 (1995): 4–6.

Haynes, Kenneth F., and Daniel A. Potter. "Sexual response of a male scarab beetle to larvae suggests a novel evolutionary origin for a pheromone." *American Entomologist,* 41, no. 3 (1995): 169–175.

Jackson, R. R., and S. D. Pollard. "Jumping spider mating strategies: sex among cannibals in and out of webs." In *The Evolution of Mating Systems in*

Insects and Arachnids, edited by J. C. Choe and B. J. Crespi. Cambridge, England: Cambridge University Press, 1997.

Kotiaho, J., R. V. Alatalo, J. Mappes, and S. Parri. "Sexual selection in a wolf spider: male drumming activity, body size, and viability." *Evolution*, 50, no. 5 (1996): 1977–1981.

Lloyd, James E. "Bioluminescent communication in insects." *Annual Review of Entomology*, 16 (1971): 97–122.

————. "Bioluminescence and communication in insects." *Annual Review of Entomology*, 28 (1983): 131–60.

————. "Firefly mating ecology, selection and evolution." In *The Evolution of Mating Systems in Insects and Arachnids*, edited by J. C. Choe and B. J. Crespi. Cambridge, England: Cambridge University Press, 1997.

Mitchell, P. L. "Combat and territorial defense of *Acanthocephala femorata* (Hemiptera: Coreidae)." *Annals of the Entomological Society of America*, 73, no. 4 (1980): 404–408.

Oldroyd, H. *The Natural History of Flies*. New York: W.W. Norton, 1964.

Otte, D. "Simple versus elaborate behavior in grasshoppers: an analysis of communication in the genus *Syrbula*." *Behaviour*, 42 (1972) : 291–322.

Oxford Scientific Films Ltd. *Sexual Encounters of the Floral Kind: Intriguing Methods of Pollination* (video). Oxford, 1981.

Phelan, P. L. "Evolution of mate-signaling in moths: phylogenetic considerations and predictions from the asymmetric tracking hypothesis." In *The Evolution of Mating Systems in Insects and Arachnids*, edited by J. C. Choe and B. J. Crespi. Cambridge, England: Cambridge University Press, 1997.

Preston-Mafham, Ken, and Rod Preston-Mafham. "Mating strategies in spiders." *Scientific American*, 279, no. 5 (1998): 94–99.

Proctor, H. C. "Indirect sperm transfer in arthropods: behavioral & evolutionary trends." *Annual Review of Entomology*, 43 (1998): 153–74.

Rice, W. R. "Sexually antagonistic male adaptation triggered by experimental arrest of female evolution." *Nature*, 381, no. 6579 (1996): 232–234.

Roeder, K. D. editor. *Insect Physiology*. New York: John Wiley & Sons, 1953.

Scudder, G. G. E. "Comparative morphology of insect genitalia." *Annual Review of Entomology*, 16 (1971): 379–406.

Spieth, H. T. "Evolutionary implications of sexual behavior in *Drosophila*." *Evolutionary Biology*, 2 (1968): 157–193.

Thornhill, R., and J. Alcock. *The Evolution of Insect Mating Systems*. Cambridge: Harvard University Press, 1983.

Tschinkel, W. R., C. D. Wilson, and H. A. Bern. "Sex pheromone of the mealworm beetle, *Tenebrio molitor*." *Journal of Experimental Zoology*, 164 (1967): 81–85.

Tuxen, S. L., editor. *Taxonomist's Glossary of Genitalia in Insects*, second edition. Copenhagen: Munksgaard, 1970.

Waage, J. K. "Dual function of the damselfly penis: sperm removal & transfer." *Science*, 203 (1979): 916–918.

Warren, John H. "Biology of *Wolbachia*." *Annual Review of Entomology*, 42 (1997): 587–609.

Wilkinson, G. S., and G. N. Dodson. "Function and evolution of antlers and eye stalks in flies." In *The Evolution of Mating Systems in Insects and Arachnids*, edited by J. C. Choe and B. J. Crespi. Cambridge, England: Cambridge University Press, 1997.

Wood, D. L. "The role of pheromones, kairomones, and allomones in the host selection and colonization behavior of bark beetles." *Annual Review of Entomology*, 27 (1982): 411–46.

Index